Acknowledgements.

I would like to thank my awesome wife Sophie for standing by myself throughout the many hours that I have had my head emerged in my laptop.

In addition to this I would like to thank my brother and sister, also my friend lee for all being my external backup centre throughout the months in which the book has been developing and for giving myself honest opinions on the book in progress!

Strangely I must thank my dog max for being there when I have had to get up and walk off the anger that has built up as I have been getting my life story onto paper. It is surprising how much supressed anger erupts when you start really thinking about your past.

Finally, I want to thank Joseph Clough, the self-help guru, hypnotherapist and NLP practitioner whom has unknowingly assisted myself through some of the darkest times of my life. When there was no one else, through his audio files he opened my eyes to the different perspectives and showed myself a new way of being in this world, he also inspired myself to write this book. He is also the inspiration for my future work as he taught me to believe in myself and taught me that it is only me in which can decide my limitations and capabilities, no one else.

In addition, I would like to thank my mum, the only mum that I have got and the only one in which I will ever have, I want to thank her for being there in spirit and I know that if she had the choice she would still be here to this day.

Thankyou mum, I love you.

In memory of Matt Newman whom sadly passed away in 2017, he was a work colleague whom even though I knew for only a very short few months touched my heart and my life, and I know that he touched many other people's lives and hearts as well. RIP Matt you will be sadly missed by many.

<u>In our darkest hour.</u>

<u>Introduction.</u>

The smell of singed hair fills my nostrils, followed by the tingling of the flame against my bear flesh, the tingling almost immediately becoming a painful burn. I grimace as I look at the skeletal figure staring back at me, tears fill in my eyes as the smell of burning skin fills the tiny hallway. The colour of the skin turns from red to a deep red, still I hold the cigarette lighter in place, until finally I drop to my knees and the lighter falls from my hand onto the cold hard tiled floor. There is now a second burn above the first one, I am in agony at this point, but I dare not cry out, its midnight and the flat walls are thin. Sitting slumped against the wall in the hall way I look around, the doors to the bedroom, kitchen and bathroom shut, concealing my behaviour from the world. Gently I touch the burn on my leg, its seeping a clear liquid at this point. "What the fuck am I doing?" I ask myself as I drag my exhausted body back to the bedroom.

Laying down in bed I pull the covers over myself, I wince as I try to lie down at an angle in which allows myself to be covered up but the burn not to be touching the covers. I grip the bedding tightly as tears fall from my eyes.

"How have I got here?" I ask myself again as I drift off to sleep my pillow wet from a mixture of sweat and tears.

That's a good question, how did I get there? In fact, how the hell did I go through that time in my life, to this one, were I am sat here writing this book in the hope to help others, whom life has beaten down to the point of complete self-destruction. I will tell you how I got here, I got here through grit, determination and motivation to make something of my life. I got here by refusing to let life beat me, no matter what.

It's time to tell you my story, my story with no filter, my story with no Alias, my story with absolutely no hidden secrets. My story with the truth, 100 per cent the truth about my life, the good, the bad and the ugly.

I will tell you my story, then I will give you the ability to access the power of you. You see you must remember something, you already have the tools within you to live life in a fulfilled way, to deal with anything that life may throw at you, all you need to know is how to use them.

Chapter one.

The very beginning of my journey.

I do not have many memories from when I was living with my biological parents, in fact most of my life up until the age of five years old is a blur. The memories I do have are, in most cases, vague and violent. But as I said, no filter, 100% truth, right?

Memory 1.

I am frozen to the spot, I can hear screaming and shouting coming from inside a room to my right. Standing in the hallway facing the front door I do not move, I dare not move, am I aloud to move? Am I in a time out? I do not know but what I do know is that the sound of the screaming is loud and is terrifying me. I suddenly hear a female scream loudly and a wine bottle shoots passed my head, the window in the top of the large wooden door makes a smashing sound and the window bulges outwards were the bottle has hit it, but it does not smash fully. I stare at the bulge in the window as I hear footsteps behind me.

After this my mind is blank, as if what happened is to horrific to remember.

Memory 2.

Walking up to the brown garden gate I place one hand on the metal catch and the other on top of the wooden frame. The paint peeling from beneath my tiny fingers as I grip the gate tightly, attempting to get some more power to force the catch open that seems to have rusted shut. Suddenly the catch releases and the skin on my finger peels open, exposing the bear flesh as the rusted catch traps it between the sliding part and the stationary part. Screaming I stare at my finger, it's trapped, I look back at the front door of the house. The large wooden door is partially open, the white paint peeling off the door. Screaming and panicked I pull back and my finger is free, leaving a small chunk of flesh in the metal catch. Once free I turn towards the house and run up the paved walkway, the garden on either side is overgrown, mixed in the thick brambles and nettle bushes are torn bin bags and pieces of sharp rusted metal, seemingly from a car. A brown settee sits near the wall of the house on the right side of the front door, but I am not looking at this, I am concentrating on my finger, there is blood trickling down my hand at this point and I am feeling somewhat sick and faint. Running through the front door I glance down at the brown carpet, then back up at the walls as I stagger into the house, the walls tainted with light brown cigarette tar. I stagger into the room immediately on the right-hand side of the hallway as you walk into the house. A big figure of man is sat on the settee, he is staring straight ahead, and he has a white and red long-sleeved shirt on. His large hands and arms by his side.

 "Dad" I say through sobs as I approach him with my blooded hand outstretched. I glance up at the women on the other side of the room, she is standing up near the settee but does not move a muscle, she looks at me her eyes sunken and deep with sorrow.

The women, she is my Mum and she smiles weakly as our eyes connect in a fleeting glance and then I look back at dad. The room spinning by now, "dad I think I am going to be sick" I say looking up at him my eyes pleading with him to help me. Grabbing my shoulder with his rough and large powerful hand my dad spins me towards the kitchen and snarls at me to "go and be sick in the bin you little shit" before forcefully shoving myself forwards nearly knocking me clean off my feet.

 I stagger into the kitchen, I am hot and sweating at this point and I feel like I am about to pass out. Glancing at the sink it's overflowing with plates and there is mouldy food on the side. I flick open the already partially opened bin and kneel by the side of it, the bin and the room now spinning. I want my mum, but I know better than to cry out when dads around.

Chapter 2.

Two years of hell.

Opening my eyes, I looked around the large room. The dark brown curtains are closed, but there is a gap where a stream of sunlight is entering and casting a strip onto the large dark brown table that is adjacent to my bed. The table is massive and seems to swallow the room, to the left of the table is a fireplace and at the end of the bed that I am lying in is a large white wardrobe that also seems to loom, at the foot of the bed. Wide awake now I stare at the large wooden table, I have no clue as to where I am, and panic starts to set in. I stare at the table which seems to loom over me like a large tree in a dark forest, as I stare at it the table seems to get bigger and bigger and closer and closer. Thinking the table is going to swallow me up like a monster in a horror movie, as the table moves towards me I let out a blood curdling scream.

So that is how my journey started in foster care, awaking in an unknown house, with no memory of how I got there and no memory of what had happened previous.

Its morning on the weekend and I have been in the foster home for a while now. I go to get out of bed when a young girl walks into my room with curly hair. She is quite a bit older than me though and a bit bigger, so I quiver a little as she stands at the end of the bed with her arms folded. I don't move as her eyes lock onto mine like homing missiles. I have taken many a pasting off this young lady by now, so I know what she is capable of. I am sat on the edge of the bed when she walks towards me, her name, Sonia. She grabs my wrists and pushes me onto the bed with force making me sink into the mattress. "You are not getting up yet, hear me?" she snarls, her warm breath on my face and her teeth visible like a snarling dog's teeth would be. I nod in agreement to terrified to speak and she turns and leaves the room.

Hours seem to pass, and I eventually muster up the courage to get out of bed. I Take myself to the landing and stop and listen for Sonia. She is nowhere to be seen so I quietly but quickly tiptoe down the stairs, into were my foster mum is standing in the kitchen. "Morning" I say as I approach her.

"Morning? Its lunch time child, get upstairs and get changed." I turn on my heel and do as I am asked. My foster mum seems angry that I am up so late, I am too scared to tell her that Sonia told me to stay in bed, yet I am angry and upset that the morning has gone. I like to spend it in the garden on the old bike. I hold back the tears as I put on my clothes, I am six years old and potentially in a lot of danger even though I do not realise it.

Most days were like this in the foster home, there was me and the devil, also known as Sonia. She seemed to love to terrorize me and it was about to get a lot worse. As time went on she found more and more ways to hinder my life until one day she put me in hospital.

It was in wales and we had gone on holiday as a "Family". There was my foster mum and dad, they were cool to be honest, I always saw my foster dad as someone whom was approachable and someone whom I could trust. My foster mum was ok I guess, she could be a bit of a witch at times to be honest, like the time she threatened to slap the back of my legs for lying to her. Even though I had not lied to her, part of me wanted her to slap my legs, I felt I deserved it just for being there, just for existing. In addition to this I had not understood the question and out of fear just said yes. It was an automatic response that I got used to using with Sonia, the response that had seemed to save my arse more times than not.

So, on this day we had decided to stay at the house. The house that my foster mum and dad had rented was a small farmhouse in the middle of wales surrounded by fields. I remember pulling up a couple of days previous, I was glad to be out of the car, I had already filled 2 plastic carrier bags with sick and was close to throwing up into a third when we pulled to a halt on the gravel driveway.

Sonia for some reason was being particularly nice to me on this day. She took a hold of my hand and smiled at me before asking if I wanted to take a walk across the fields with her.

I was unsure of the way that she was behaving, it unnerved me that she was being so nice. As we walked towards the field, there was a barbed wire fence that blocked us off from getting into it. We looked but could not locate a style. Sonia found some looser fencing further down the side of the field away from the house, she stepped over it before pushing half of the fencing down with her foot and lifting the other half up, so it was low enough for me to step under and over. As well as this she held my hand and helped me carefully climb through. I winced slightly as the wire touched the back of my inner leg. When I was in the field Sonia took a hold of my hand and started to walk with me across the field, by this point we were still in view of the holiday cottage and if our foster parents were looking out of the window then they would be able to see us both.

As we got further and further away she started to pick up her walking pace but keeping a tight a hold of my hand. As the cottage came out of view she walked quicker and quicker whilst keeping a tight hold of my hand. I asked her to stop as at this point I was running and could not keep up.

"Stop, stop, please" I begged as I ran flat out for as long as I could as her hand tightly clasped around mine refusing to let me go. It was no use, the more I begged the harder she pulled, and eventually my legs gave way. Spinning around Sonia glowered at me angrily. "I can't keep up" I whimpered as I looked back up at her. Her eyes were dark and menacing. She looked like she wanted to kill me.

 "Get up!" she snarled dragging me up by my arm roughly.

 "We are going back, you're a useless piece of shit" she snarled as she clasped my wrist tightly and ran back towards the fence, with me attached to her like a piece of meat trailing behind. I tried my best to keep up, but it was no use, my legs were too small and did not have the power to keep me upright and running at the same time, so she dragged me most of the way back. As I saw the fence approaching I felt slightly relieved, it meant that the running would be over soon, and my lungs would hopefully not feel like they were going to burst. When we arrived at the fence Sonia let go of my hand and threw me to the floor forcefully. As I picked myself up she hopped over the fence and glowered at me before demanding that I "Climb over, and quickly!!" She was not holding the barbed wire down for me like she was a few minutes age and she was also glowering into the back of my head waiting for me to get over it. I did not understand the rush, but I was prepared for her to give me a wallop. She didn't, what she did was much worse, as I was pre-carelessly perching on top of the barbed wire fence she grabbed my arm and dragged me over it. Consequently, it left my leg trailing behind and the fence ripped it open like a tin opener, slicing along the inside of my thigh near my knee the depth of the barbed wire itself, which was about half an inch deep. I screamed at the top of my lungs as I fell to the floor grabbing a hold of my leg tightly, Sonia realised what had happened and looked at me with a shocked and frightened look on her face, her hands clasped tightly over her mouth she took a step back and looked at my leg, the deep gash open and leaking blood. Sobbing I looked away from her and back down at my hand that was at this point saturated in my own blood. I moved my hand which revealed a 3-inch-long and 1-inch deep gash in the inside of my thigh just above my knee, it was wide open and there was a small pool of blood beginning to form on the gravel that I was lay on. Suddenly Sonia grabbed my t-shirt with her powerful hands and pulled my face close to hers.

"There is an old bike around the back of the building, you got on it when I told you not to and you sliced your leg on the metal frame, if you tell them the truth, your dead, get it?" I felt sick at this point and faint, I could feel the colour draining from my face as I looked back at her, my eyes red from crying and my body feeble. I nodded weakly in agreement, because I believed her and because I was terrified. Then without warning, Sonia grabbed my hand and dragged me across the gravel driveway and towards the front door. I could not stand or walk so I screamed in agony as the stones ripped into my knees and sliced at my shins, there was a trial of blood leading from the fence to the large brown front door in which we landed. By the time we had got to the front of the holiday cottage my knees and shins were bleeding and there was numerous cuts and grazes in addition to the large gash in my leg. My foster mum came to the door, by this point I was hysterical. "Calm down!" she said sternly kneeling to get to my level.

"I said, calm down!" she shouted pushing her finger hard into my stomach. I looked at her in disgust as I tried my best to calm myself down. She glowered at Sonia and asked what had happened as she glanced down at my leg.

"He was playing with an old bike around the side of the building" she lied. "I told him not to, but he would not listen, Joe fell and sliced his leg on the rusty frame."

"Didn't you?" Sonia snarled pushing her finger into the side of my arm from the back, so her mum could not see.

"Yes" I replied quietly, looking down at the floor.

My foster mum took one look at Sonia, a look that said a thousand words. Part of what was communicated was that she did not believe for a second that is what happened, and I could see in her eyes that she was going to find out the truth even if it meant beating it out of her. Something which I had seen happen to Sonia before, and deservedly.

As we drove to the hospital I placed my head into the carrier bag and wretched, the smell of vomit that was already in the bag overpowering, I was travel sick at the best of times, but this time not only was the motion of the car making me ill, but there was the added warm blood that was trickling down my leg, the pain was a dull ache. Every time we went over a bump however the skin on the open wound would seemingly slap together creating an agonising pain that made me cry out.

We came to a halt outside of the hospital, I was glad of the cool air hitting my sweaty face as I hobbled out of the car with the aid of my foster mum and dad. I don't remember having to wait but I do remember hobbling into a large room with a green bed in it. My foster mum sat by the side of me and held my hand as I lay on the bed and a woman in a white uniform studied my leg.

"I bet that's sore? You're very brave" she said softly smiling at me as her eyes locked onto mine making me feel at ease. Gently yet firmly applying pressure to my leg and holding it in place she told me that there was going to be a slight stinging sensation but then it would be all over. I looked at her slightly confused but that confusion suddenly turned to fear as I saw the doctor walking towards me with a large needle. Another nurse appeared seemingly out of nowhere and pinned me to the bed from behind as my foster mum held onto me firmly, the nurse whom was holding my leg pinned it in place, I screamed as I watched the man place the needle into the cut, it seemed to take him forever to inject the clear liquid into my leg, the pain was sharp, and intense.

"Hey" said a voice. I looked down, tears streaming down my cheeks. The lady in the white uniform was looking at me. "You're doing really well, we are nearly done now" she said softly. She had blonde hair and she was very pretty.

"You hold your mum s hand and look at you mum or at the ceiling for this bit" she said calmly. "We are just going to put some little stitches in your leg, so we can close it up, the stitches will help it heal, and then you will be free to leave." She explained.

I felt a slight pressure on my leg and then heard a loud click. After a few seconds, I looked down as the lady was bandaging my leg, the metal clamp sticking up out of it.

The rest of the holiday was somewhat difficult. I could barely walk and when I did try to the bandage and staples rubbed against the inside of the other leg causing a somewhat itchy red mark. The stitches themselves also itched and trying to get down the inside of my leg under the bandage without my foster mum screaming at me to "stop messing with the bandage!" was like trying to complete something out of mission impossible.

If I am being honest my foster mum and dad were cool, it was Sonia that made my life hell. That was one of the worse beatings I had received off the her, there were many more. She used to take pleasure in slyly destroying my toys and then trying to get me into trouble with my foster mum. Like once one Christmas when she took a hold of my new felt tip pens and rammed all of them in front of me into a large pad of paper purposely destroying the nibs. When I went to go and tell my foster mum she strangled me and bounced my head off the wardrobe like a basketball, before setting the boot in when I was lay on the floor in a heap. The house was a massive house, it was 3 stories high and had loads of room inside and out. So, when one person was at one end of the house and the other person was at the other end if I was taking a beating then it was not heard. This she used to her full advantage.

She used to also like to bully my little sister as well. I was 6 when she hospitalised me, regularly kicking the shit out of me. My sister would have been 2 years old. I remember her putting my little sister in her high chair and then dangling a massive toy spider in front of her and laughing as she screamed in terror frantically trying to get out of the chair. I just stood there, to terrified to move or do anything, knowing my arse would be handed to me if I did. That is something in which I have never fully forgiven myself for, even though I was only 6 at the time.

Chapter 3.

Soul destroying news.

It was a weekend again, Saturday from what I could remember. I had eaten breakfast and was walking past the living room area after being in the cellar with their biological son. He was a joiner and an awesome bloke, I loved to watch him work, I found it amazing how he could turn pieces of wood into furniture, turn nothing into something.

"Joe, can you come in here please?" I heard my foster mum ask softly.

As I walked in the living room her husband was sat across from her on the large chair that was part of the settee set. I looked up at my foster mum whom gestured for me to sit on her knee. As I approached her, I noticed that her eyes looked sad, teary, as if she had been crying, and she seemed solemn in body. I had seen that look before, it was the look that my biological mum had often worn, but she always used to churn a smile out for me though.

She lifted me onto her lap. Sighed deeply before talking "Unfortunately we have some bad news, your mum died last night, and your dad has had to go away for a while, so you are going to stay with us whilst we find you a new home"

I just sat there looking at her whilst the words hit me like a steam train. I do not remember much that happened directly after that. It's a blank, I do however remember spending most of the day outside, on my own riding around on an old bike that they owned. It was warm and sunny outside, and I rode around and around in circles in the garden, up and down the path and back up again. My little mind trying to process the information, trying to process the fact that my mum was gone, forever. I was 6, and my life was a mess.

It was a few days later that my foster mum approached me and passed me a picture of my biological dad, he was stood near some railings with a wall behind him, and someone had taken a photo of him for me. He was smiling but he seemed unhappy in his eyes. He was a young fellow, in his 20s. I remember looking at his stubble and remembering how he used to rub his chin against my cheek, it used to make me giggle when he did that, so why was he not here now? I still could not comprehend what was happening or what had happened, all I knew was that dad was in prison and mum was gone, forever.

So that was it, I was to be put up for adoption. It is a strange thing when you get placed up for adoption, it's like when farmers go and look at cattle and pick and choose which cow they would like. That's basically what happened to me and my sister. It happened so fast.

I was walking towards the back door of the house when my foster mum stopped me in the doorway. She explained that there was "Going to be some people that were going to come and visit me and my sister, they were a man and a woman, and if they liked us, and we liked them then we could live with them instead of her.

I was somewhat excited by her news, since the only thing on my mind (Excluding losing my mum and dad) was getting away from Sonia. Don't get me wrong, when she was not around, life with my foster mum and dad was awesome. I played for hours in their large back garden and used to love picking the peas out of the pods that we collected at the back of the house. Also, I used to love helping my foster dad and his son do 'Manly work' it made me feel grown up.

Chapter 4.

Meeting my adoptive parents.

So, it was not long after my foster mum had told me about the visit with these strangers that it happened. It was summer, and it was a sunny day, I was doing what I usually loved to do in the summer and at weekend, I was in the garden of my foster parent's home when my foster dad walked out into the rear patio area from the kitchen, he was a short and rather rounded fellow, he was followed by a very large man with ginger hair. He was massive, he walked with confidence and his hands were gigantic, he was a lot taller than my foster dad and mum, he was also a lot taller than his wife, whom followed behind. She stopped near the edge of the patio near my foster mum, she smiled from afar and looked nervous and she stayed very quiet. She reminded me of my real mum, she had always been in the background, somewhat beaten down.

Mark walked over to myself, he was smiling and seemed very friendly for such a gigantic bloke.

"Here" he said as I watched him approach. "I'll kneel down, so we are similar height" I don't know whether he saw fear in my eyes as he approached or whether it was because he knew of the horrific things my biological sperm donor had done but either way it immediately put me at ease.

I do not remember much of the conversations that I and Mark had that afternoon, but I do remember play fighting with him on the grass in the garden. I felt safe in his giant like hands as he threw me up in the air and then caught me again. He knelt so that he was at my level when I threw myself at him just knowing that he was going to catch me and gently wrestle me to the ground, throwing me hard enough so that it was fun but soft enough that I did not hurt myself. For a good couple of hours, I forgot about the world, everybody else seemed to disappear into the background and myself and Mark connected and on a deeper level, we were both caught in the moment.

I was gutted when it was time for them to leave. I did not want Mark to go, he was cool, he was calm, and he made me feel safe, feel loved and wanted, just for them 2 hours he made a massive impression on me. He made me feel like nobody could hurt me ever again. I wanted him to stay and protect me, protect me from Sonia.

I do not remember interacting with his wife on the first visit. She stayed in the background. I should have taken that as a warning, especially as she was behaving like my biological mum had behaved, when she was around my biological dad.

I was excited to hear that Mark was coming for a second time with his wife a few weeks later, and Sonia was suddenly being nice to me, all the time. I do not know whether it was due to her feeling guilty for how she had treated me in the past or whether it was because she loved to hate my guts and was sad to see me go.

So, after about 3 visits, one where Mark and his wife took us out on their own to MacDonald's. Us being me and my little sister, and another occasion being when they took us out again but this time to their house. It was a farmhouse in the middle of nowhere, a little village called flash. I remember Mark pulling into the large drive way and helping myself and my sister out of the massive 4x4 vehicle that we were in, it was a big black car from what I can remember.

Mark had bought me, and my sister presents, I cannot remember what my sister got but I was given a batman. It had a little button on the back and when you pressed it the wings opened. He had given it to me after showing myself and my sister around the farmhouse and our bedroom. The farm was massive, it had a large field at the front and the farm itself was a long building with a large front porch. The house had a massive garden and there was plenty of space to run around in. As you walked in through the porch you then entered a kitchen which had dark rough quarry tiles down as the flooring and wooden counter sides. The living room was at the back of the house and the dining room was in the middle. To the left near the dining room was a staircase that led up to a large thin and long corridor. At the end of the corridor was mine and my sisters room, it was a large room and there were 2 beds, one for me and one for my sister, the room had been separated. One side was mine and one was my sisters.

My favourite part however was not the fact that they had a farmhouse, horses and fields, it was the fact that they had a tractor, an orange one that I could drive around the farm, it had a large dirt shifting bucket on it and it had no gears, just a forward and backwards peddle, Mark walked by the side of me as I drove it up and down the massive farmhouse driveway. I fell in love with the Kubota, I fell in love with Mark, he was awesome.

After the three visits, my foster mum approached me in the kitchen back at her house. She knelt in front of me and took a hold of my hands and asked in a soft and seemingly saddened voice if I liked Mark and his wife.

"Yes!" I said excitedly. Why would I not like them? They were kind to me and they were awesome. They lived in a big house and had a tractor, I was sold, what was there not to like?

"Ok" said my foster mum smiling weakly, she looked upset in her eyes, they were watery as she spoke, and her voice quivered a little.

"Do you want to go and live with them? It means you would no longer live here with us?" she asked as she wiped her eye that was now seemingly leaking.

"Yes!" I said excitedly, I pretended I did not see how upset she seemed, but I had noticed. At the same time, however I needed to get out of there, away from the Sonia and this was my escape route.

Chapter 5

The real mark.

I do not remember leaving my foster parents home, I am guessing it was that distressing that my mind has blocked it out, just as I do not remember how I got from my biological parent's house to my foster home, the only difference is that on one occasion I awoke up in a strange bedroom not knowing where I was, and on the other I awoke in a bedroom that I was sharing with my little sister and I felt safe and loved.

Mark and his wife lived with me and my sister for a year in the house that we were originally adopted into. It was good when we lived in that farmhouse. Not only was Mark half decent as a father figure his wife was also very hands on with me and my sister, she was always doing things with us when we were not at school and when Mark was at work. I remember one day myself and Marks wife made a plaster of Paris batman together and laid it to set in a red mould. I was so excited in the morning that I could not wait for me and Marks wife to open the batman, that morning we peeled back the plastic, when we did it revealed batman and I set to decorating him. I kept batman for years after that, all the way until I was 19 years old.

Unfortunately, Mark was not a very nice person, and as far as I am aware still is a nasty bully. I started to find this out from a very young age, when I realised that he had another side to him.

Money in the wrong hands can be a nasty thing if you allow it to take a hold of you. If you allow it to change your behaviour. Mark was a well-off man he had his farmhouse in a village called flash and he also had his wife and now children, he had a successful car business and was somewhat doing well for himself.

Our relationship was OK when we lived at the old farmhouse in flash and one day he even took time out to take me for a bike ride. We went for miles, it was a red-hot day from what I could remember, and we must have been out for 3 hours of the afternoon, it was like when I had first met him at my foster mum and dads. He was nice to me and seemed to genuinely want to spend time with me.

I and my sister wanted for nothing financially and we went on many holidays, Menorca, France, America and Italy. You name it we went. My sister had her own horses and anything I wanted I got. Money was never an issue as Mark has always worked hard. He has also always been a bully though, and has always bullied himself to the top.

As time went on something changed, and as I got older for some reason Mark seemed to resent my presence. He made me feel as though my existence was a sheer inconvenience to him and whenever he got the chance he would shout at me, his favourite trick was to do it in front of people, I think this gave him a sense of power, made himself look and feel powerful.

The school I attended when living with Mark was small, very small, when I was there, there was 20 students in the whole school, so small in fact that it nearly closed.

Mark for starters thought he knew it all, he thought he knew everything about everything. So, when I came home from school with homework he was quick to take it out of my hands and tell me exactly how to do it, and it had to be done his way, if it was not done his way then he would become angry and shout me down, looming over me as he shouted, forcing me to do it his way, even if I explained to him why it was wrong. This then resulted in me getting into trouble from my teacher as my homework was always wrong, when I eventually told the teacher what was going on at home he became quiet and told me not to worry about it. I was confused as to why he had not offered to help me resolve the situation with my parents. Instead he turned into a coward and did nothing, so the cycle continued.

Chapter 6.

Living with a bully.

So, even though as I have previously highlighted, some of the aspects of living with Mark and his wife were great, the holidays and the fact that we travelled a lot. There were a lot of things that were not, in fact there was a lot of time in my 13 years spent with this pair of (A-hem stay professional) not very nice people that I hated.

Not only was I horrifically bullied at school, secondary school especially, but I was also bullied at home.

Life was tough, one day, after class, I was sat in the corridor waiting nervously for the bus to pull up. The corridor had benches on either side and the library was near to where I was sat. Directly opposite me was the double doors onto the playground near to where the bus normally pulled up to take me home.

I kept glancing nervously up the corridor to my right, I knew it would not be long before the lads would be on their way. There was a fat kid called Joe. He was part of the "tough" group of lads, also known as thugs, or even cowards as they hunted their prey in packs, like wolves.

The ring leader Adam had stirred so much trouble that he had now organised a fight between me and Joe. After school. Looking to my left and right, then back in front I made sure I had all the exits covered so I could leg it. I needed the fastest escape, my plan was the bus, but it was not here yet.

Suddenly I heard whooping and shouting, I looked up to my right and there were about 8 lads walking towards me. Joe and Adam in front, the other 6 kids at the back. I didn't move, I was a dead man, there was no way I could outrun 8 lads and there was no way that I was going to beat Joe in a fight, he was 3 times my size and was bought up in the rough parts of town. I was well and truly fucked.

I subtly slid my bag off my back and sat back down again, Joe approached me, and stood over me with his arms open wide. The other lads close behind him.

"Come on then! Let's have it, prick" He said stood over the top of me with his arms open, the stench of body odour filled my nostrils as he got close to my face, with him nose to nose, his breath smelled like rotting ham.

I tried to stand up, but my legs were shaking that much that I sat back down again. "I do not want to fight you" I said my voice shaking as I spoke.

Next thing I know I am looking at the floor and can't breathe, Joe has got me in a head lock.

It took a while for my brain to catch up with what was happening, it was like a voice in my head started to scream at me. "Joe, you are in a fight, defend yourself." I grabbed a hold of Joe s arm and pulled at it, just enough to give me room to breathe, at this point the room was starting to spin a little and I could see the other lad's feet, so I knew they were stood close and ready to set the boot in if I did go down. I knew that no matter what I had to stay on my feet. Reaching up Behind Joe s back I grabbed at his hair, but it was to short and there was nothing for me to grab, so I stuck my finger up his nose instead, he let go of me.

 I ran fast towards the red framed door, I knew that if I went to the playground I would be beat even more, so I tried to get back to the art room where I had just come from as I knew the teacher would still be there. As I grabbed at the door handle 2 powerful hands gripped me from behind and rammed me against the glass hard, they then spun me and threw me across the floor like the hulk. I slid like a ten-pin bowling ball and hit the wall on the other side of the corridor. As I scrambled to my feet Adam came out of no were and landed a sickening blow to my gut. As I dropped to my knees, I could not help but notice the disturbed grin on Adams face as he watched me roll forwards onto the highly polished floor face first, determined not to give up I scrambled back to my feet, I needed to get out of this situation. As I stood Joe came at me head on and landed several body blows to my gut and face and a side kick to my ribs, as I dropped to the floor for a third time a teacher appeared and stopped the beating.

So that was one of the many pastings that I received in my school years.

However, Mark was more of a psychological bully, at least with the lads at school I knew what I was getting.

So, for example, there was one night in which I will never forget, I was working on a project for school, it was an English piece basically we had to write a story based on the crystal and the seven dimensions, and we were to make it up, we had been asked to write a section on one of the characters for this day. As I knew how much of a twat mark could be I spent more than 1 hour writing an A4 piece that before I could hand in to school he had to check. I made sure that it was the neatest piece of writing I had ever done. I also knew that he expected the top line to be double under lined with red pen and if it was not he would screw it up, or mood dependant scream at me to do it again. I was sat on my desk and had spent the last 30 minutes checking whether the work looked good enough or not and whether Mark would approve of it,

I was somewhat sweating as I stopped on the top of the stairs and triple checked the work before I took it down for him to look at. As I rounded the corner into the kitchen I could feel the taste of iron in my mouth as the thumping of my heart in my chest sped up, as I got into the living room I looked across at Mark whom was sat in his big chair in the corner of the room. Sticking out his hand Mark gestured for me to bring the work over to him. As he took it I could feel my arms sweating as he scanned the page, he was not in a good mood, he rarely was but this time I could just tell.

"It makes no sense!" he snarled holding the paper in front of me like it was something he had just wiped his arse with. "But the teacher…." "No buts" Mark interrupted drawing a red line straight across my work and then scribbling down the page.

"Dad!" I said in disbelief, my voice shaky, partly due to anger and partly due to being upset. "The teacher said that is what we had to do!" I explained.

"Oh well" He replied. "If that is what she said to do then you will have to redo it then!"

I remember walking up the stairs that night seething. I wanted to kill him, I wanted him dead. He did that every time I had schoolwork to do, he 9 times out of ten made me redo it or destroyed it.

It gave him power, he was a control freak and a bully, but I always felt like the one that was in the wrong. The one that was good for nothing, the one that was useless. At the time I did not realise, but I was starting to believe that I was a useless boy whom was nothing without mark.

Unfortunately, that scenario was a far too regular occurrence in our house.

You see not only did Mark control my school life, my homework to the extent where I had to show him everything. But he also controlled what I did before and after school and we had strict routines I and my sister did. (I am writing this and there is a mixture of anger and disgust going through my body but at the same time I want to laugh at the ridiculousness of it all.)

In the morning, I and my sister were expected to get up and clean out the horses that Mark and his wife owned. There were four of them. I would then go in and make my lunch for the school day ahead and then go and start marks car to make sure that it was warm enough for him for when he got into the car. Or to defrost it in the winter. This created a problem though because if the car had a different alarm system then what I was used to I would set off the alarm and I would get shouted at. I would then have to make a cup of tea for Mark and his wife and take it up to their bedroom to awake Mark in the morning.

If I spilt the tea on the wooden stairs, then I would get shouted at. I also had to make sure that I awoke him half an hour before we left for work/ before he dropped us off at the bus stop so that he had enough time to get ready. Also, he had to have his keys and brief case put in the car for him otherwise he would complain if it was not in the car.

Then we would go to school, I would be dropped off outside the pub, which is where the bus would collect me. My sister would be dropped at Marks wife's mums as she went to a different school to me.

On returning home from school the first thing we would be expected to do was to go back in and get changed and then clean out all the animals again. Once this was done it was upstairs to start our homework. I used to hate it, the anticipation of waiting for Mark to get home from work, I could see out of my window when he pulled up outside the house and he got out of his car, his ginger hair bobbing about on his fat bulbous red head. I used to pray that he would get into a car crash and die, I used to hope he would ring and say that he was delayed at work so that he did not come home until I was in bed asleep. I hated him with a passion, I didn't always hate him but as time went on and as I got older we drifted apart to the point where we did not speak. We were more like slaves then children to Mark and his wife.

Chapter 7.

When things start to turn ugly.

So as the years went on mine and Marks relationship turned more and more rocky. Mark wanted complete power over every aspect of my life even to the extent that he had decided before I left school what my career path was going to be, which as far as he was concerned was going to be working for him.

I knew this was a bad idea, but I felt like I had no choice, whenever I did tell mark that I did not want to work for him it was combated with.

"Well what are you going to do? If you do not want to work for me then what actually are you going to do" he would then stand over me with his arms folded and a stupid grin on his face.

"If you do not work for me then you are going into the building trade!" he would say with his arms folded.

"Come on then Joseph! What is your job going to be!?" he would ask getting agitated that I was not answering him straight away but also seemingly in his element that I was not able to answer his questions.

That's basically how it would end, I would just say ok then I will work for you, knowing that no matter what I said I would be overridden. It was not as if Mark was doing me a favour by giving me a job either.

It was all for his own personal gain, or at least that is certainly how it looked. He was paying me a measly wage of £325 pounds a month for 6 days a week at his garage and 1 day a week at home, so no matter what, I could not get away from him and was always working with him. It works out at about £1.20 an hour.

It took me up until the age of 18 to start to realise what was going on here. Mark had full control of every aspect of my life, just what he wanted. He controlled my income, my phone bill and car insurance were both payed for by him. My income was that low that I could not move out even if I wanted to, my phone bill was a listed phone bill so every number I rang was listed and Marks wife made me write down whose number was whose, so she could see how many times I txt and called people and whom it was I was talking to.

So basically, no matter what I did I was controlled, Mark mentally made me feel not worthy enough to leave his garage and even told myself that he did not trust me to work anywhere else that is why I was to work there. There was many a time that he would tell me that I was "a useless cunt, a thick twat, and things like I was acting like a cunt at a christening, or I was fucking stupid" Its laughable some of the creative names that he came up with for me but it still smarts even to this day, writing this makes the pit of my stomach knot with anger, it's good for my dog max though when I am writing, he gets plenty of walks because I have to keep going out to calm down again.

I do not want to make the whole book about Mark but as you can imagine he has had a massive negative impact on my life, so I will choose a couple of things to tell you about, the ones that have had the most impact on myself. The things that I believe are what contributed on a large scale to me believing that I was not worthy, useless and good for nothing.

This happened when I was younger, just turned 17 years old, Mark and his wife had holiday cottages that they rented out, they were situated straight across the driveway from the house. One summer holiday I and my younger sister became friends with the kids that were on holiday with their parents. It was that much of a memorable event that the eldest girls name was Becky and I can see her face as I am writing this, she is whom I became friends with and the youngest was Amanda I think, she became friends with my younger sister.

One evening Becky had been invited to our house and was sat on top of the bed covers in my bedroom, she was watching a movie with myself, I even remember the film, Jeepers creepers. Now I am not going to lie, she was a good-looking girl, even though she was 1-year younger than me. She was 15, very close to turning 16. I was 17 at this point remember, just turned 17. On top of this my younger sister was in the bedroom sat on the floor with Becky s sister and they were playing with her Barbie set. In Marks house there was a toilet on the first flight of stairs, and next to my bedroom on the second flight of stairs in the hallway there was a bathroom.

(In that bathroom myself and my sister were not allowed to use that toilet, we were to use the downstairs one, we were also not allowed to have a bath, the excuse being that my toe nails would scratch the bath, we were only allowed a shower. Mark had also told myself that when he had built the shower that was going to be in the outside shed then I was to use that one not the one inside the house.)

So, you had to go past my bedroom door to go to the bathroom. As I was sat on the bed Marks wife came up the stairs, I thought nothing of it as she walked past my bedroom door and into the bathroom to "Use the toilet". I even said, "Hello mum" as she wondered past. So, to say that I was shocked when Marks wife went back down the stairs and he started to yell at me to "come down the stairs immediately" was an understatement.

When I got down the stairs Mark instructed me to "Stand there!" pointing with his large fat finger to an area in front of the table, I watched as Becky and her sister walked out through the front door as they had been instructed to do so by Mark. As the door shut behind Becky Mark exploded.

"Joseph! She is 15 you are a fucking idiot! Its paedophile behaviour, you are a paedophile if you behave like that!" Mark screamed slamming his hand on the kitchen table, his face turning a red colour and spit showering from his mouth as he spoke.

I was confused and frightened, I looked at Marks wife, she was stood in the corner of the kitchen glowing at me her arms folded. Mark stood opposite me, the kitchen table in between me and him. My sister as confused as I was stood by the side of me.

"Dad, what are you talking about? I've done nothing wrong?" I protested.

"You know exactly what you have done!" Mark bellowed. "You were under the covers with no top on when your mum went to the bathroom!" "That's paedophilic!!" "You were kissing her!"

"Dad, what are you talking about? We were sat on the bed yes, but we were sat on top of the covers, watching jeepers' creepers, my sister was there the whole time!" I said pointing to her.

"I was" she said. "And he was just watching T.V with her."

"Are you calling your mum a liar!" shouted Mark, slamming his fist against the table again this time making it shudder.

"Dad, we are telling the truth!" I said glaring at Marks wife in disbelief. She knew I was telling the truth, I did not understand why she was doing what she was doing,

"Bitch" I thought to myself as I looked back at Mark.

"Your sister is in charge tonight, me and your mother are going out." Growled Mark as he stormed out of the house with his wife.

I must have stood in the same spot for a minimum of 30 minutes after they had gone, confused as to what was happening and what had just happened. I was sickened to the stomach that I had been accused of such a disturbing crime. Even more so when I found out that Mark that night had told his friends how I was a paedophile. I was already known as Marks useless son, now I was known as Marks useless son, the paedophile.

Chapter 8.

As I got older, there was as I am sure many people can relate, from both sexes, many meets with women in which will stick with me for as long as I live.

There is 2 in which stand out for myself.

One was with an older woman, I like older women, always have.

I met her when I was at work, she was a pretty lady, it was also clear to see that she used the gym a lot.

The difference with this lady and many of the others is the fact that she was nice to me, she took the time to listen, she made me feel at ease with her and what you saw was what you got. She also did not always have her head buried in her phone which really grinds my gears.

She was also not shy, not shy I think is an understatement. It was not long before myself and this woman ended up in the bedroom. Back then, me trying to work my way around a woman was like an apprentice trying to work his way around the mechanics of a car. Like you must start somewhere but there were way too many fiddly parts for me to comprehend.

Eventually after about an hour her patience ran out and I ended up face down whilst she whipped me mercilessly with a thick leather belt. Now I don't know if you have ever been spanked with a belt before, none the less from a woman that has arms like Arnie and frequents the gym, but it hurts, a lot.

 The spanking did 2 things, it opened an acceptance to myself, to accept myself for me and not be ashamed of my kinks and fetishes, kinks and fetishes that were created in that one moment, (But now as I write this, I question myself to if they were always there, deep seated and she just helped me bring them out in the open. I remember my dad beating my brother and sister, maybe this is something that has contributed to the feeling of 'needing' or wanting to be punished) so much so that there were a few times after that in which she visited just to put me across her knee to correct any unwanted behaviour. Strangely it made me feel more confident with women also.

And then there was Sarah, now she was a character.

 So, I was in college at this point when I met this lovely individual, in fact it was a collage "Friend" of mine that I had met upon my bricklaying course that said he had a "friend" that needed a boyfriend, or was looking for a relationship and that she was a "Lovely women".

 So, after getting her number and a few messages back and forth we organised to go out on a date.

It was a wet night in Wilmslow as I pulled up near the curb where I had organised to meet this woman. Noticing a very tall and muscular figure wearing a dress with her back to me, I drew forward a little. Curious, but at the same time saying to myself, "That cannot be her that cannot be her" As I stopped the car the "Women" turned around.

She was about 17 stone of pure muscle, her shoulders were wide enough to be a wrestler, and I shuddered as she marched toward the van. Swinging open the passenger door she bent down and stuck her head in.

"Are you Joseph!?" she bellowed.

My eyes opening wide with fear I managed to squeak a "Yes"

"Good" she said as she threw her lumber some body into my small van making it rock violently as she slammed the door shut. Glowering at me she bellowed. "Were have you fucking been? Its fucking pissing it down out there!" pointing her Shrek like finger towards the window, and leaving a large smudge on the glass.

Looking around it suddenly dawned on me that the estate that I was on was rough, very rough. There was smashed beer bottles and glass everywhere, graffiti up the walls and dark alleyways and bushes, I was half expecting someone to come out of the bushes and ambush me. Apart from Sarah, it was quiet, to quiet.

"How the fuck am I going to get out of this?" I thought to myself as I glanced over to where Sarah was sitting. She was like Arnold Schwarzenegger in drag, she took the whole of the passenger side of my van up and she was that heavy that it leaned to one side and stayed leaning to one side.

"Sorry, the traffic was bad" I lied.

"Its fine, just make sure you are on time next time" she said sternly pointing her fat finger in my face.

"There will be no next time" I thought to myself as I drew away from the curb.

"The names Rob" she said holding out a hand.

"Rob?" I questioned as I held out my hand to shake hers, her hand was that big that it engulfed mine.

"My name is Sarah, but I prefer rob" she said as I turned away from her turning my attention back to the road.

"Okay, were would you like to go?" I asked with as much positivity as I could muster, even though every nerve in my body told me to get out of the van and run as fast as my skinny little legs could carry me.

Down the road, my local pub, she demanded as she took out her tobacco and started to role a fag.

"It's not a bad pub, it's just reopened, someone got stabbed last week, and they died!" Rob told me almost gleefully as we drove towards the destination.

Pulling up outside of the pub I felt nervous. I was not the best with knives for a starter, and the area we were in was like something out of a Jason Stathern movie, when he pulls up in a dimmed car park and 6 guys come at him out of nowhere. That was the atmosphere.

As we walked towards the dimly lit pub my heart started to beat hard in my chest and I started to feel weak. I opened the door for Rob gesturing for her to enter the building.

"Aren't yaw a gentleman!" she said loudly slapping me hard on the back of my shoulder sending me flying across the room and taking the wind out of my lungs. I stayed for a few seconds bent double with my hands on my knees to catch my breath before looking up.

There were some seriously big powerful and rough looking men in here, and there were some seriously powerful and muscly women as well. And then there was Rob, whom I was with, she looked like she would put up a good fight.

"What do you want to drink?" I asked her sheepishly as I made sure that I did not make any eye contact with anybody knowing that I would be dead if anyone started on me.

"Pint of Stella! Cheers Love!" she said slapping me hard on the shoulder again and pointing towards the pump.

I looked at her in disgust as she walloped down the beer like a filter whale taking a mouthful of water in.

Taking a seat at one of the tables I looked up at Rob and smiled. I was trying my best to think of the quickest and most polite way to get myself out of this situation. Not only that but I did not want to upset her as I knew that she would kill me if she decided to kick off.

Sat across from me her elbows resting on her knees, her legs open she wasted no time in asking me about my personal life.

"So what yaw experience then, yaw know, in the bedroom?" she asked looking at me directly in my eyes.

"Oh shit!" I thought to myself as I repositioned myself nervously in my seat.

"Err, none to be honest" I whispered as to make sure that no one overheard.

"Ah right, you're a fucking virgin then are yaw!!?" she shouted.

The pub went deadly silent. I felt myself going red as everyone turned to look at me. One big muscly bald guy glanced over at me and then turned away chuckling to himself. He knew that I was way out of my fucking depth.

Suddenly it dawned on me what I had to do. I pushed myself back in my seat and clutched at my stomach.

"Arrh" I groaned. "I don't feel well!" I said looking up at Rob with pleading eyes.

"I think I need to go home" I told her as she got up off her seat with a concerned look in her face. I felt sorry for her to be doing this but at the same time the other option was to just leg it and drive off and I did not want to leave her stranded at the pub.

As we pulled up outside the road to where I picked her up less than an hour ago she thanked me for taking her out. I shot back in my seat as she leaned forward to kiss me, as I shot back Rob placed her powerful hand on the back of my head and pulled me towards her forcibly and kissed me, I turned my face sideways, so she got my cheek instead of my mouth. After holding me for a few seconds in her Shrek like hands she got out of my van and before shutting the door poked her head in. "Don't be fucking late next time" she said before slamming the door.

As soon as the passenger door was shut I locked the van doors and drove off like a rally driver wheel spinning away from the curb. As I drove down the duel carriageway I vowed never to take Rob out again.

Chapter 9.

Finally leaving.

I could write a book alone on some of the women that I have dated, but I am sure that at some point the stories will be covered in my mental health page and blogging page on Facebook. (Joe Williamson/writer/blogger/vlogger/self-help guru). So, I won't prattle on for too long!

As I got older, life got more and more difficult, Mark seemed to resent me more and more and would seem to pick fights with myself at every chance that he got.

It got to the point when I hit the age of about 20 years old I did not go home after work until midnight if not later, (At this point I was a bricklayer), I would go straight from work to the pub and have tea there until I knew that everyone would be in bed when I got back home so that Mark could not have a go at myself for something that he plucked out of thin air. In the morning, I would then get up at 5 am and make sure I had left the house for 6, I knew for a fact that Mark and his wife would not be up at that time so if I was gone for then, then there was no arguments or conflict.

I got around weekend by starting early at his garage and finishing for 11 am. I would then either go to the pub or go and visit Marks wife s mum for the day. Sunday, I got to the stage where I refused point blank to work at home with Mark. I would either refuse to help him and sit in my bedroom or go out driving and or visit Marks wife s mum.

Eventually I had had enough and decided to start actively looking for somewhere else to live.

It was not long before I had found myself a flat. It was in the middle of a local town near to where I lived with Mark. The land lady lived in the flat above the one that I was to rent, the flat was small, but it was big enough for myself. It had a back and front door and a small kitchen and living room area with 1 bedroom and a small toilet and bath area. For me it was ideal, it was an escape, I needed to get away from Mark and his wife and this was my chance.

After meeting with the land lady of the flat I rang Marks house phone from the pub and left a message saying that I would be moving out at the end of the week and that I did not need or want his assistance. Basically, it was a warning to leave me alone.

On moving day, I rushed down to the garage and washed all the cars and had done my jobs by 11am.

Mark had not spoken to me all morning until about 10:30 am when he stopped by the side of the car that I was cleaning. I looked at him and waited for him to speak. He was glaring at me, trying to intimidate me and thinking of something clever to say.

My mind flashed back to the conversation Mark had had with his wife the night before.

"Don't worry, Joe will not last a week on his own, he will soon come back!" I heard Mark say from the bathroom upstairs as I lay in bed, awake.

I glared back at Mark from the step stool that I was stood on, knowing that he was going to try and down talk myself, but I was determined not to let him change my mind, especially after last night's conversation. I was going to prove him wrong no matter what.

"Well you are moving out then?" Mark said smugly crossing his arms as he spoke.

Without speaking I nodded my head to answer yes, I was not giving him the satisfaction of hearing my voice shake.

"Well good luck because you are going to need it, I can predict your future now. You are going to fail, you are going to live the rest of your life in a council house eating beans on toast." He said looking at me disapprovingly and waiting for me to respond with his arms folded.

"Ok" I responded as I turned my back on him and continued to wash the top of the car. I felt him glowering at the back of my head as I continued but I refused to turn back around, after a few seconds I heard him turn and walk away.

It was time to leave, I had driven back to the large farmhouse that I had lived in for the last 10 years and I was in my bedroom placing my life long belongings into boxes. I took them downstairs and placed them into the back of my van. Marks wife sat in the living room silently, the women I had called mum, I walked in the living room and held up some wooden coat hangers and asked her if I could keep them for my clothes.

Silently she nodded yes.

"Thankyou" I said as I turned to walk away. I could see she was upset, she had tears in her eyes, but she had had her chance. So, had Mark. I had warned her 6 months previous that if Marks abuse did not stop then I would leave, I had told her that I was not dealing with it anymore and that I was getting older and I needed to live my own life meaning less restrictions from her and Mark, for example not being expected to spend the only day I have off working while Mark tells myself how much of a useless cunt I am.

"Key" Marks wife said in a stern voice as I turned to walk out of the living room door.

"What" I recoiled turning back to look at her.

"Key, if you are living on your own you no longer need this house key, and I do not want it to get stolen if you are moving to that rough town"

Turning I stared at her for a second, not really believing what I was hearing.

"Sure" I said forcing a smile, I did not want her to see the lump that had formed in my throat and how hurt I was, I did not know myself why it upset me so much, but it did. Passing her the key I turned and walked to the van with the coat hangers.

After it was loaded I closed the back doors and took a second to look around. I had had some good memories here. I looked across at the field that myself and my younger sister used to play fight in when we were little, I smiled, nostalgic for a moment.

Closing my eyes, I then heard Marks voice. "Joseph, are you fucking stupid, how many times do I have to tell you? Followed by the whack across the back of my head. The mixed rush of emotions of wanting to cry and wanting to tear his throat out all at the same time entered my body. Opening my eyes, I looked around, it was then that I realised just how many ghosts this farmhouse held. The negative ones more pungent than the positive.

As I scanned the driveway I half expected Marks big 4x4 to come screaming up the driveway and he to attempt to stop me from leaving, no sign of any vehicle, nothing.

I got into my van and drove it up the driveway and to the top if the drive, as I got on the level I slowed down, second guessing myself.

Sitting there for a second I tried to remind myself of good times, give myself a reason to stay.

Looking towards the field in front of me I looked at the large wooden gate, I saw Marks wife walk in front of myself carrying a dog lead and a horse riding crop. Glancing down to the left I saw myself stood there, frozen to the spot, ten years of age. I watched in horror as the collie dog yelped as Marks wife mercilessly whipped the dog with the horse riding crop, he was tied to his lead, so he could not escape. It was because he would not stop chasing the hens, so instead of paying to have him trained she whipped him viciously.

Without hesitation, I put my foot on the accelerator and pulled to the bottom of the driveway. I had had enough, and it was now or never. I knew one thing for sure, I was not coming back.

Chapter 10.

My Darkest days.

It was about 5 months into living on my own that things started to become hard work. The first couple of months were great, I had freedom, there was nobody telling myself what I should and should not be doing. The thing that was tough, there was nobody, I was alone, I went to work alone, and I came home alone. It was just myself and my thoughts.

My mentality was not the best, you see when I was on the farm I was living with the constant barricade of negativity, constantly being told that I was not good enough and that I was not going to succeed in life, especially if I did not follow someone s path and do exactly as the individual wanted myself to do.

When I was going home to the flat that I lived in, I was alone, with the thoughts of not being good enough. Not only this, but I was proving to myself that I was not good enough time and time again. At this point I was hooked on sex lines, I was hooked on pornography, and I was beginning my journey of self-destruction. Alcohol had become my best friend and my worst enemy at the same time.

I was still on the building site at this point, but I had handed my notice in where I currently worked and was attempting to set up my own business. I stupidly ended up working for one of Marks friends.

This did not help my situation, I jumped from the frying pan into the fire. The person I was working for clearly had no idea how to run a business as nearly every cheque he gave myself bounced and he treated myself worse than Mark did. Because of the way that Mark treated myself and because he was friends with him he clearly saw me as his whipping boy.

Soon I was in a cycle where I was feeling not worthy to be alive let alone do anything else, as not only was I working for one of Marks friends whom relayed my every movement back to him, but he was also verbally abusive to myself.

At one point, he threatened to throw roof tiles at my head if I "didn't fucking hurry up!" even though I was exhausted, I was working that hard that I was nearly physically sick as it was so how he expected me to hurry up any more than I was doing was somewhat beyond me.

It got to the stage where I was so nervous about going to work that I felt ill every morning before I went, but at the same time I was too scared to not go. When I got back from work I would drink neat gin straight out of the bottle and then fire up the computer for my dose of porn. Following this I would then pass out on the kitchen or bedroom floor before getting back up the following morning and repeating the process. Get dressed, go to work come back and top up on alcohol.

I can't remember what night it was that I did myself harm, I do remember though that it was a night in the week. It was like any other night, I got home, placed the heavy tool bucket down by the side of the washing machine and painfully walked over to the fridge in the corner of the kitchen. The green gin bottle clasped tightly in my hand I twisted the lid off and swigged out of it. As I walked over to the settee I felt a mixture of guilt and relief, guilt for drinking even though I had promised myself I would stop and relief for being able to get my hand on the bottle. The mixture of feelings ran through my body stimulatingly as I slouched down onto the settee.

I glanced over at my computer, it was in the place where I had left it last night, I took another swig out of my bottle and just sat there staring at it, I had promised myself that I was not going to drink, I had also promised myself that I was not going to watch porn either.

The computer seemed to call to me as I got up and walked over to it, it was like I was in a trance as I neared the breakfast bar table. Sitting down I rebooted the laptop, before I knew it, it was 1 am in the morning and I was still sat there in a trance like state watching a woman lash the skin off another women s back with a long whip.

Laying myself down into bed I laid my head on the pillow and thought about how stupid and pathetic I was. Self-hatred and loathing seemed to seep through my veins as I lay there tossing and turning trying to sleep but being unable to.

About an hour went past before I found myself wanting to do myself harm, again it was like I was in a trance as I stepped out of bed and searched my bedroom for something to hurt myself with. I had never had this impulsion before and certainly no thoughts like this, it seemed to come out of the blue, as if someone was telling me to do it. Like a voice in my head, but not a voice in my head at the same time, I was lost, confused, scared and alone.

Searching frantically, I find an elastic band, wrapping it around my leg I flick it a few times, biting hard on my finger to silence myself I wince as the elastic band whips the skin leaving another red mark. It's painful but not enough, looking across my room I spot my cigarette lighter on the side.

The smell of singed hair fills my nostrils, followed by the tingling of the flame against my bear flesh, the tingling almost immediately becoming a painful burn. I grimace as I look at the skeletal figure staring back at me, tears fill in my eyes as the smell of burning skin fills the tiny hallway. The colour of the skin turns from red to a deep red, still I hold the cigarette lighter in place, until finally I drop to my knees and the lighter falls from my hand onto the cold hard tiled floor. There is now a second burn above the first one, I am in agony at this point, but I dare not cry out, its midnight and the flat walls are thin. Sitting slumped against the wall in the hall way I look around, the doors to the bedroom, kitchen and bathroom shut, concealing my behaviour from the world. Gently I touch the burn on my leg, its seeping a clear liquid at this point. "What the fuck am I doing?" I ask myself as I drag my exhausted body back to the bedroom.

Laying down in bed I pull the covers over myself, I wince as I try to lie down at an angle in which allows myself to be covered up but the burn not to be touching the covers. I grip the bedding tightly as tears fall from my eyes.

The next day I awoke early in the morning, about 5 am. I winced as I peeled the bedcover off the open wound on the back of my leg. Dragging myself into the bathroom I started to run a cool bath, sweat was pouring from my body and I felt shaky and faint. I breathed in deeply as I lowered myself into the cool bathwater, allowing it to soak the wound, the burning sensation eased as I rested my head back onto the cool plastic of the bath. I thought about all the things that I had done over the last 4 months, how much money I had wasted on phone sex lines, thinking about it most of the time it was not to use them for what they were designed for, it was to just hear a women s voice on the end of the phone. I liked women, older women, mainly because even though I did not know it then, but I wanted a mother figure desperately in my life, but I couldn't have one, the one I had been assigned by social services was fucking useless with no backbone, and my real mum was dead.

I closed my eyes as I lay there in the bath, the water now going cold, it felt good, the wound was soothed and if I got out I knew that it would start burning again.

As I lay there I made a life changing decision, and decided to stick to it. No more self-harm, No more sex lines, and no more porn. I then thought "well what if I fail? What if I cannot do it?"

"If you fail you could end up dead!" a little voice popped into my head, seemingly out of nowhere. The wakeup calls that came out of nowhere.

When I eventually got out of the freezing cold bath it was about 6 am, I gently pulled up my underwear and trousers pushing them with my hand, so they did not slide across the wound, the wound that was now beginning to sting again. Opening my fridge, I looked for some food, there was fuck all excluding some bread that was starting to go mouldy. I scraped the mould off with my knife and placed 2 slices into the square white toaster. Without thinking I opened the fridge and reached for the nearly empty gin bottle, unscrewing the cap I placed the bottle to my lips and tilted my head back, as the alcohol hit my mouth I made a seal around the bottle with my lips and dribbled it back into the bottle.

"Come on! You are an idiot!" I scolded myself as I threw the bottle into the bin and frantically looked around the flat for any other alcohol that needed to be thrown. Today was a day of change, today was the day that I needed to rid myself of my own demons and only I could do that. As I heard the toast pop up I picked up the laptop that was on my breakfast bar, walked into my bedroom and slammed the top shut before kneeling by the side of my bed and sliding it under there as far as I could get it. There would be no more porn.

I stopped as the laptop slammed against the back wall of the bedroom under the bed. My eyes became fixated on my hunting rifle, the neatly carved handle and the adjustable sight perfectly fitted together, it was beautiful, it was my protection, it was positioned and loaded in reaching distance so that if someone broke in I could reach it without getting out of bed. Realising that I had not checked my armoury I systematically proceeded to go through my flat, I checked under my pillow, my heavy weight training bar still there accessible with ease as well as the loaded air rifle. Sliding open the top drawer I glanced at my 4-inch lock knife, the blade exposed and ready to use. Checking in the hallway I checked the corner, my heavy spirit level placed just out of sight but accessible to myself. Finally, I checked under the settee, the large carving knife easily accessible to myself just in case someone broke in and beat me to the ground, I had every eventuality covered.

To explain the rifle, in fact to explain what led to myself feeling the need to arm myself, here is what happened. I had been living in the property alone for four days, it was a Thursday night and I felt particularly unsettled, so I stayed up until about 1 am watching a Jeanne Claude Vanne Damme movie. After it had finished I took myself to bed and lay down.

I awoke suddenly to the sound of hushed whispers seemingly coming from inside of the kitchen. I sat bolt upright in the dark. Terrified, "How many were there? Had I left the door open? Where they armed?"

My heart pounding hard in my chest I grabbed the nearest thing to me that I could use as a weapon. My weight training bar, gripping the cold metal in my hands I twisted the bar tightly between my fingers as I sneaked out of bed, tiptoeing in the dark across the cold black tiled floor I stopped near the door to my kitchen, the whispers became louder.

"Try that one" A strong Liverpudlian accent whispered through the dark. Realising that the voices were coming from outside I tiptoed to the kitchen sink near the back door, my heart seemed to stop as I heard the distinctive sound of the golden coloured door handle squeak as it was depressed from the outside and a loud thud reverberated around the room as someone from outside rammed their shoulder or foot into the door, clearly trying to break in. I stood there gripping the bar tightly and frozen to the spot, now in a cold sweat, my legs and arms shaking, terrified. "Thump, thump" the bottom of the door seemed to dip inwards as a stood there watching it intently, my eyes now adjusted to the darkness.

"Thump"

"Who the fuck is there, come on then fuckers" I shouted, suddenly, the words uncontrollably flying out of my mouth like water down a waterfall. My arms and legs tensed as I scrambled for my keys to unlock the door, not thinking clearly, I placed the key into the lock as I heard footsteps running off into the distance. The metal bar tightly clenched in my hands I ran towards the noise of the back gate as I heard it slam against the brickwork.

As I got into the street I scanned it for signs of life. I had gone from being frozen with fear to so angry I was ready to fight. Looking down I realised that not only was I in my bear feet but the only thing that I was wearing was my underwear, accompanied with a weapon. Suddenly realising how much trouble I would be in if a patrol car was to drive past I ran back towards my flat and got myself inside. The rest of that night I was too angry and frightened to go to sleep. Instead I turned on all the lights in the flat and lay down on the sofa, fully clothed with my metal bar hugged tightly against my chest.

As I lay there I contemplated going back to live with Mark. I did not want to be alone, I was scared and lonely, it was also cold, and the heating in the house was shocking, shocking, meaning it did not work.

Chapter 11.

One of the most stupid things I have done.

So being honest and as you have already gathered, I have done some seriously stupid stuff in my time. One of them was obtaining the rifle that I slept with under my bed, loaded.

When I was living it the flat I was horrific with money, and made some horrible decisions, not once, but on numerous occasions. In this instance I had purchased a van on a whim, just for the fuck of it I don't know. After a few weeks of it being stuck in my lockup and me having to pay extra for it being there with it having no MOT tax or insurance, I had put it for sale on the internet when I received a phone call from a potential buyer.

The man had a somewhat strong accent, my gut instinct was screaming at me to just hang up the phone. Something was not right but as always, I tended to ignore that instinct and it got myself in some seriously potentially dangerous situations.

It was a Friday night and I got into my car at about 09:30 pm, it was winter, and it was dark and cold, I made my way out of town and towards the lockup that I had hired over the last 6 months to store my tools in, and the items that I bought and sold. I had agreed to meet this man here at 10 pm, and he was meant to be alone. As I pulled up to the large metal gates I got out of my car and punched the code into the keypad. I was nervous and felt that something was not

right as I watched the gates slide open. Pulling into the large lockup I pulled up by the side of the brick wall onto the gravel parking.

Looking down at my phone I read the message.

"We are here"

"We?" I thought to myself as I gingerly got out of the vehicle and made my way around the corner. As I got to the gates I felt my heart start beating hard in my chest as I saw the large yellow transit van under the dimly lit streetlamp waiting for myself to let him in. Punching in the key pad the gates opened and the van drove through, a guy about my size and build driving.

"Alright lad, I notice there are cameras everywhere, we need to park in this corner mate, out of the way of the them" he said as he drew forward and right underneath the cctv camera so that it was not recording his van.

Jumping out he walked towards me confidently holding out a hand for me to shake.

"This the van?"

He asked pointing towards the escort van that I was selling.

"I thought you said there was just you?" I questioned as the passenger door of his transit opened and 2 what I can only describe as heavies stepped out and stood behind the small guy with their arms folded like 2 body guards.

"Mate, its ok they are err, my err, my brothers, they come along for the ride" he lied looking around to see if there was anyone else around.

"Shit, shit, shit." I thought to myself as I took a step backwards.

My hands became sweaty as I looked up at the CCTV camera.

"That thing is going witness my death" I thought to myself as I watched as the smaller guy looked around the van, his heavy weight "Brothers" not moving, eyes trained on me.

"IL take it, it's a nice van, let me show you the gear" he said gesturing for me to follow him to the side of his van.

As the van door slid open I wiped my hands on my trousers, they were at this point dripping with sweat and I was somewhat anxious. I stepped away nervously as I felt my eyes opened wide, samurai swords, powerful air pistols and rifles were laid across the back of the van completely covering the floor. Near the front there was a box full of knives, daggers and knuckle dusters. Some of the knuckle dusters were bladed, curved into fancy angles, double edged, like something out of a blade vampire movie.

"Look at this" The smaller man said smiling as he spun around sliding a very large dagger out of its casing. The edges of the blades paper thin and extremely sharp looking. Taking a step back I panicked as my way was blocked by one of the large men. I was alone with 3 unknown men, one holding a dagger and the other 2 stood directly behind me. Not moving I just stared straight ahead at the guy with the knife, my heart pounding and my hands up by the side of my head in a submissive stance. "what the hell is he going to do next?" I thought to myself, convinced that I was a dead man.

He walked towards me, the dagger in his hand, the blade pointing towards myself, at this point I was stood on the foot of one of the large men, his steel toe capped boot I could feel beneath my shoe, digging into the centre of my foot. Waving the knife at one of the lads stood behind me he burst out laughing.

"Give the kid some space lads, your frightening him" he gestured as he walked around to the side of me placing an arm around my shoulder he guided me back to the van and told me to get in. Looking behind me, I watched as the lads did as they were asked. The bloke holding the dagger sliding it back into the sheaf.

Picking up a sheet at the back of the van he exposed 3 powerful air rifles.

"Choose one of them buddie, take your time" he said calmly"

Nervously I picked up the one with a sight on it. It had a beautiful carving in the handle.

"I knew you would pick that one lad, she is a beauty, isn't she?"

He said slapping me hard on the shoulder before passing me a gun case for it and 2 x packs of pellets.

As I drove home I thought about how stupid I had been, they could of beat me to a pulp, stabbed or shot me, emptied my locker and took the van including my car. I would have been powerless to stop them, I was outnumbered, and they had a van full of weapons.

When I got inside the flat I made sure that the curtains were shut and pulled the rifle out of the gun bag that I had put it in. Snapping the rifle, I pulled a bullet out of one of the metal containers and snapped it shut. "Click" Looking down the scope and the sight itself I suddenly felt powerful, safe and protected. If someone broke in now, I was going to shoot them right between the fucking eyes. I aimed the gun at the back door and imaged in my mind someone walking through the door, then bang! I watched them as they dropped to the floor.

And that is how I ended up with a loaded rifle under my bed.

Chapter 12.

Time for change.

Ok so back to page 56, the day I decided, no alcohol, no porn, no more sex lines and no more self-harm. I had been stupid, and it was time to change. I did not want to be the person I had become. I was better than this, deep down I knew that, I just needed to prove it, I needed to prove it to myself.

It was about a week after making the life changing decisions that I went to see a good friend of mine, he lived down the road from myself. I visited him regularly and he came to see me regularly.

On this occasion I had not only gone down to see him, but I had gone down to also use his internet to check my social network accounts. You see I had had internet, but I had been cut off, I was foolish with money, with a mixture of spending stupid amounts of money on phone sex lines and alcohol, and with a mixture of not being paid regularly it had ended up with myself completely broken, I was receiving daily phone calls and letters from debt collectors. They were continuedly sending threats of debt recovery, "Legal action pending" or "If you don't respond to this letter we will enforce our collection activity with bailiff's" "We are going to send around enforcement agents". The letters became a normality after a while, I went from being fearful of receiving a letter to being completely unaffected by them, I didn't even read half of them, straight in the bin they went.

Stepping out into the rain I made my way down the road to his house. He lived in a 3-story town house across from a garage.

I cannot remember what we talked about that day, I cannot remember much other than the event that would change the course of my life forever. As I sat crossed legged on my friends couch I logged into my account, readjusting myself I pulled at the part where my self-inflicted injury was on my leg. It was healing but it was sore, mainly due to it not being left to heal properly, I had not covered it up over the last week, so it had been rubbing against my jeans, consequently leaving it still fleshy and susceptible to infection. Even though it was itchy and painful I was careful not to pull at it too much as I did not want him noticing that I was in pain and asking questions.

I clicked on the unread message icon that was glowing red, it read.

"Hey, I do not know if you remember me or not, but I just thought I would say hi, we dated each other a few years back."

I looked at the message blankly, repeating the woman's name over and over in my head, "Sophie, Sophie, why can I not remember?". I thought to myself as I sat looking at her name. "She must have the wrong person, no one would want me" I thought to myself as I sat there staring at the screen, my mind completely blank.

Jumping up off the settee I grabbed my head with both of my hands as thousands of images flashed through my mind, attached where old emotions, which were now suddenly as raw as if it was yesterday.

Suddenly I was in a trance like state as I followed Sophie up the wooden stairs at her parents' house, she was wearing her skater girl type trousers, brown in colour, as I followed her I thought about how nice she smelled as the perfume seemed to engulf my senses.

Looking at Lee and then back at the computer I clawed at my head trying to physically remove the painful memories that were engulfing my mind and body.

Again, I was deep in a memory, like time travel, reality was no longer reality. It was a cold dark night and Myself and Sophie Walked together hand in hand, through a field and onto a country road that led up into a small village. There we sat together on a stone wall, we watched the lights of the town below glimmer as the last of the sunlight disappeared, 16 at the time, both of us forgetting our troubles and just being in the moment, together, one of the rare moments that was just me and Sophie, a rare time together without some psychopath interfering.

Breathing in deeply I gripped onto the window ledge in Lee s bedroom, I did not know it then, but I was having flashbacks, and they were coming thick and fast.

Suddenly I was back in Sophie's house, we were in her bedroom and were lying together on her floor in fits of hysterical laughter, one of those magical moments when you don't know why you are laughing, but you both are. Smiling I closed my eyes as Sophie poked my nose with her finger, opening them I found myself stood on the curb outside her house, staring into her eyes, tracing every part of her face with my finger and pocking her nose back, gently with my finger saying bop, we held each other whilst waiting for Mark to come and pick me up, waiting for him to come and take me away from her. Watching her as I got into the large 4x4 I followed her with my eyes as she walked away down the dark alleyway. I did not realise it then, but that was the last time I was going to see her.

"Why! Why has she contacted me now! I have done everything to try and forget her!"

I shouted as I walked around his living room somewhat lost and confused, emotions that I had buried for years were now as raw as the day we were split up and Mark refused to let me see her anymore, As raw as Gordon Ramsey's language.

Looking through her Facebook I felt my heart growing heavy as I scrolled through the photos of her stood with a man, and a child. She had left me behind, I was her past, yet at the same time she had found me?

"Why the fuck is she doing this to me?!" I said to lee in disbelief.

It took me about an hour to decide what I was going to do, I was to reply, I had to reply, there was a reason she had contacted me, and I could not miss this opportunity to find out why.

I will never forget the first time that I saw her again, it was in January 2010, I had spent the afternoon tidying my flat and making sure I looked decent before she arrived. I was that anxious that I could not eat, I felt sick and excited all at the same time.

As I walked through the back door of the small flat I felt the cold of the winter seep through my skin and chill me to the bone. Breathing in deeply I stopped at the back gate where we had agreed to meet, I peered over the top of it, there she was, as beautiful as ever, just as I had remembered her but a little older. Opening the gate, I called her name, spinning around she smiled at me and opened her arms for a hug. As I embraced her I was suddenly 16 again, there was no awkwardness and no loss of connection. It was like we had never been apart.

A relationship flourished from nothingness after that, Sophie moved into the flat with myself and so did my stepdaughter, (One whom I love and consider as my own daughter.)

Chapter 13.

Fast-forwarding a year.

Not only did I allow that little flat to destroy me to the point of near complete self-destruction, but it also in a very short space of time nearly destroyed my and Sophie s relationship. It went from being a place that I loved, to a place I hated, loathed and detested. It was a symbol of financial destruction and emotional negativity.

Me and Sophie were verbally fighting, we had no money and everything we did seemed to not work.

There is one night in which I will never forget, we were sat on the leather settee in the living room, my eldest daughter was only about 2 years of age and it was late at night. We had had to sit her with us as the land lord whom lived above us was drilling late into the night, with him being above us it was scaring her and even though we had asked him to stop he ignored our requests.

I was sat on the left side of the settee and Sophie was on the right, the eldest daughter in-between us both, she had finally drifted off to sleep. I looked at Sophie, she looked exhausted, the lamp in the corner of the room shone dimly, the flat cold. We had no lightbulbs left excluding that one and we had no money to be able to pay for anymore. The electricity meter had nearly run out of money, so we didn't dare turn on the heating.

I looked at the crooked brown front door, then my eyes scanned my flat, the blinds to the front window thick with dust and twisted. I looked back at Sophie whom was sat on the settee her hand resting on my eldest daughter's foot. I was hungry and cold, exhausted, I did not know what to do to get us out of the situation in which we were in. I was the man of the house, yet I felt incapable of protecting and providing for my family, I was at the lowest I had ever been, I had been ok with letting myself down, but I was not ok with letting my family down.

My mind scanned back over the last 12 months as I tried to figure out where it had all gone wrong. I thought back to my porn addiction and all of the money that I had wasted on sex lines and online scams that "Promised to make you a millionaire in 6 months! Not a scam but give us £200 first."

I even recall a conversation I had had with an American man, he was trying to get £60 quid out of me in a promise to make me a millionaire. It was at a point in my life just before Sophie moved in in which I realised that I was being scammed and put the phone down on him.

I then thought back to the job that I had at the time. It was working for one of Marks friends whom had not only threatened in an underhanded way to "Pay me a visit" because I had spoken out about him bouncing 60 percent of the cheques in which he gave me, but he had also been threatening to throw roof tiles at my head and the such whilst I was working there.

I understand that I had not helped myself during the last 12 months, but the people around me had not helped either, in fact they had made things ten times worse.

That night it was with a heavy heart that I laid my eldest daughter in her travel cot in our room, I was disappointed in myself, I was angry and hurting.

Life had become impossible, I did not know what I was going to do, I could see no way out.

We finally after plenty of arguments and heartache found a place that was cheap enough and big enough for us both to rent, a little 2 bedroomed house. Literally walking distance from the flat that we had been existing in. The day that we moved into there was a small stepping stone. I had got myself a new job. I was due to start the week after we had moved into the new house, and mine and Sophie s relationship was somewhat stronger for getting out of that destructive environment.

After a week of living in the house life seemed to be taking a turn for the better. Even though I still had debt collector letters coming through the door, I had however got used to them now, they had become a normal part of my life.

However, I will never forget the first time in which I opened the envelope containing a letter from a debt collector.

The Big Red letters seemed to jump off the page at me.

LEGAL ACTION PENDING

DO NOT IGNORE THIS LETTER.

YOU OWE £400.

PAY IN FULL, IMMEDIATELY.

As I read the words I remember sitting down on the cold hard tiled floor in the flat, my head spinning, and my hand was shaking as I read the letter over and over. I felt immediately sick and somewhat faint.

"Legal action? Was it illegal to be in debt? Were they going to come and break my legs like they do in the movies, was I going to get arrested?"

In the flat I was intimidated by the letters, in this house however I laughed at them, screwed them up and threw them in the bin. I had had letters like this for months and nothing had come of them, they were just empty threats with no real-life consequence? Or so I thought.

Chapter 14.

A dark entity in the house?

It was 5 weeks we had been in the new house, we had gone from existing to living, I had been in my new job for 4 weeks. Many aspects of our life had started to change for the better, even though I knew that the date for the pay day loan in which I got the house deposit with was due soon, I had no intention of paying it back, so I didn't care.

Even though things were a lot easier, life was still in many ways tough, and there was something weird going on in the house.

My oldest daughter would not settle in her room at night time at all. We used to have to sit with her until she went to sleep and pray she did not wake up until the morning, otherwise she would refuse to sleep in there at all.

One morning at 3 am I awoke suddenly and sat bolt upright in bed. I felt my body lift from the bed, I was weightless as I found myself floating and drifting along the dark wooden flooring, across the carpeted landing and towards my eldest daughter's room where I stopped in the doorway. I could not move but I wanted to, there was a dark hooded figure bent over my daughter's bed, staring at her, watching her, it wanted to hurt her, I could sense its intention, but I could not move, I fought with my arms and legs as I tried to force myself forward, but I was glued to the spot.

Suddenly I awoke properly, I awoke biologically, jumping out of my bed I ran fast, I heard Sophie shout something at me as I ran through the wooden barn type door, but I ignored her and leaped over the landing hallway. Slamming into the closed bathroom door as I tried to round the corner into my daughter's room. Hitting the floor hard as I crumpled in a heap I dragged myself to my feet I ran into her room and skidded to halt by the side of her bed. The first thing that I noticed was how icy cold the bedroom was. There was no one there but I was terrified, my daughter was ok, but it felt like there was someone there, there was defiantly a male presence, or at least it felt like there was one. Sophie shouted from the bed, "What are you doing? What is wrong?" Ignoring her I glanced around the room and checked the window. There was a strong smell of cigar smoke that seemed to linger in the bedroom and the room was freezing. I tucked my daughter up in bed with her covers to make sure that she was warm in that room.

I turned and walked back into the landing, immediately noticing the difference in temperature and the cigar smell disappearing, the vision of the man imbedded in my mind. A dark shadow stood over the top of her bed.

That was one of many unexplained happenings. One night it was about 2 months into living in the small terraced house, number 73 it was. I was sat in the living room with Sophie and my eldest daughter. It was about 7pm at night and we heard a sudden smash of glass as if someone had broken in through the back door of the kitchen. I jumped up off the settee and ran towards where I had heard the sound. As I rounded the corner into the kitchen I looked down at the orange tiles on the floor and stopped in my tracks. It was icy cold again, and there was glass everywhere yet the door to the back patio was still intact. I looked over to the shelf that was opposite the door, I then looked back at the door, the door had a mark in the middle of the bottom panel were something had clearly hit it with force. Sophie had 3 very large glass sweet jars on the shelf. They were that heavy that I had to use both hands to lift one of them up as a then 22-year-old man.

As I studied the glass it came apparent to myself that the glass had not simply fallen off the shelf, it had clearly somehow been thrown. From the shelf to the door was about 3 feet strides, so if the sweets jar had simply fallen off it would have smashed right below the shelf, but it did not, it had hit the back door with force and then smashed on the floor near the door. All of us including the cat that lived with us at the time were in the living room at the time of the glass smashing. There was simply no explanation of how the glass jar had been thrown across the room with such force. No-one else was in the house and the back door was locked.

It was a few weeks after this incident when I was walking down the stairs and I heard Sophie shouting my name from the kitchen, followed by,

"Why have you done that?"

"Why have I done what?" I retorted as I walked into the dining room agitated at her shouting.

"That" she said pointing towards the table angrily.

On the table was a newspaper that I had bought for her the day previous, I had left it there overnight as in the morning she liked to read it whilst eating her breakfast. Sophie had been downstairs for all of 2 minutes before I had followed her down so there was no way she could have done what she was so angry about. As I walked towards her I leaned in and inspected the magazine more closely.

"Well" she said folding her arms whilst glowering at me over the top of her glasses.

Every page of the magazine's top right corner had been folded perfectly into one another stopping at exactly the advertisements for the rented house section. So, when you opened the magazine it opened as if it was one big page straight onto the house section.

"Why the fuck would I do that?" I said laughing thinking that Sophie was pulling a weird prank or something.

As I studied the newspaper more closely I realised that the corners of it had been folded that perfectly that it would have taken a good 30 minutes and plenty of concentration to do such a task.

We stopped and looked at each other for a moment, realising that it was neither of us that had done it.

The only people capable of doing such perfect folds was myself or Sophie, and it was not either of us. My eldest daughter at the time was in nappies so it certainly was not her.

Again, we were both baffled, who had done it? How had it happened?

Chapter 15.

Hell, on earth.

A few weeks had passed since I had started working at the nursing home, even though I was working hard, money was tight, so tight that we were literally living pay cheque to pay cheque and we were just about putting food on the table. I was getting paid pittance for the job that I was doing and mine and my wife s working hours were clashing massively, with no one trustworthy or reliable at the time to look after my daughter it was practically impossible for us to get a good working week in each, without there being some row or disagreement over what the hell we were going to do with our daughter.

Mark was no longer on the scene and Sophie s mum continually let us down. It was unbelievable the amount of times we turned up at the agreed time to drop off our daughter at her house, for her to just turn her away at the door, leaving one of us not being able to work. Some of the excuses that she came up with were ridicules, such as "I can't today as I am going to town" or "I can't today as I am decorating". It was hit or miss as to whether she would look after her granddaughter without turning her away or making some stupid excuse as to why she couldn't. When she did look after our daughter she expected to be paid for it. In addition to this there was also a very high risk that she would phone half way through my wife s working shift and shout down the phone, demanding that Sophie immediately leave work and come and collect our daughter as she was not looking after her.

In addition to this I had gone from enjoying my work to hating it. It had become a horrific place to work, a place of abuse, neglect and mistreatment, carried out by some of the most despicable people I have ever met.

I was employed as the cleaner there, my job was just that. To clean. I spent the first few weeks enjoying myself, I did my job to the best of my ability and I did as I was asked to do by my superior. One of the requests I was advised was for my own good, it was to keep 2 carer s happy. Pat and Lynn.

Lyn was a rather tall lady whom also had a bit of weight behind her, she was also the mother to the devil. Pat.

For the first few weeks I did as I was advised to do, and I avoided Pat and Lyn like the plague, mainly for self-preservation.

Until that was, that I started to notice things, things that I could not just leave by the wayside and ignore.

There was an old lady whom I will never forget, she was bed bound and could hardly move, but she did used to roll a little and she was a chatty little lady. I used to look forward to cleaning her room as we used to always have a good chat, even if it was the same conversation. I can hear her voice now as I am writing this.

"What is the time?"

"What is the weather doing?"

She would ask me this every 30 seconds, and every time I would smile at her and tell her the same answers over and over as I was cleaning her room.

One morning I went in and the room had a very strong scent of faeces. I said good morning to her and explained that I would come back to her room later as I had forgotten something. At the time I came out of the room Pat was walking past and I told her in a very low tone that her room had a strong scent of poo and that she might need changing.

"Ok" she responded and then walked off. 1 full hour went by and she had still not been changed, so I told another carer.

This went on from 10 am in the morning and at 2pm in the afternoon the lady had still not been changed and had been lay in her own shit for 4 hours straight. I was furious, and upset at the same time.

The care staff were all sat in the lounge area drinking tea and laughing loudly when my personal manager came up to myself. She said that she wanted to talk with me in private and that it was urgent.

As I followed her to the laundry room I felt myself becoming more and more agitated, my nose was itching, and my temper was bubbling underneath the surface.

As I sat down on the stool situated near the washing machine in the laundry room, she explained that the carer whom was in charge had come to see her. She had told her to pass the message on to mind my own business and that the care staff were more than capable of doing their jobs.

At that I exploded into a fit of rage, standing up I threw my arms up in the air and began to shout.

"So, what the fuck are we supposed to do then? Leave her lay in shit for hours on fucking end and not say anything to anyone? Would you lay in shit for four hours!"

My manager at the time put her hands in front of her and nodded her head in agreement.

"I understand, and I completely agree with you, but there is nothing in which we can do, that is how they are"

She replied calmly yet silently, almost afraid of the care staff overhearing the conversation. It was clear that she had been treated this way for years, it was clear that she did what she could for self-preservation, it was clear that the care staff were vicious bullies and purposely did things to hurt other people. Pat clearly was a bully, she used fear as a weapon, she had all the staff running scared to stand up to her. The upsetting thing was that a lot of the residents whom were vulnerable feared her to. She was clever with it though as well, the people whom were more able she treated with respect and kindness, they thought that the sun shone out of her arse.

By doing this she created herself complete protection, staff that feared her, residents that feared her, and residents that protected her because they thought that she was an amazing woman. This being due to their own experience of her, one of patience, kindness and love. She was a professional, a professional abuser.

That night I went home angry, very angry.

Grabbing myself some plain paper and a pen I began to scribble.

After about ten minutes I had a hand-written letter addressed to the manager at the time. It was readable, but the writing had jagged edges and was scrawled in line with my mood.

Writing to the manager and talking to her in line with the safeguarding strategies I had been taught were not working, I very quickly understood why it was that, so many people feared Pat and her mum. It was not long before I started to receive wrath of the care staff, nor was it long before the care staffs abuse towards the vulnerable residents became worse and more violent. I am still uncertain to this day whether it's because I was looking for it and had noticed things, or whether it was because I had started to take a stand that they became more aggressive and brazen with their behaviour.

One of the incidents that shook me to my core took place only a couple of days or so after the first one. I was polishing the side rails that led down the corridor and I heard Pat shouting from a room at the far end of the corridor, in the bedroom to the right.

"Look at you! You are covered in it, you are covered in shit!"

Immediately I stopped what I was doing and looked towards the room and listened.

"I am sorry, I, I, I, am sorry"

The frail and frightened old woman's voice seemed to haunt the corridor, as she responded to Pat, the person whom was meant to be protecting and supporting her.

"You dirty old women!" I heard Pat snarl as I stood frozen to the spot, listening.

I heard the old lady apologise again, then begin to weep, it was heart wrenching.

"Right! You're going in the shower!"

Suddenly Pat burst out of the room dragging a commode with a frail, weeping and fully naked old women on it, covered in her own faeces, no towel, no nothing.

I just stood there, my mouth open watching as she dragged the terrified women down the corridor at speed whilst shouting at her that she should not have shit everywhere.

Yet again I found myself in the manager's office, reporting these acts of disgusting horrific abuse. The woman was terrified, and her face, the face of complete terror will never fully leave me.

Nothing was done, again.

Also, it was obvious that Pat knew that I had reported her, as shortly after this incident her and her mum stopped talking to me and decided to make my life hell.

On this day it was my turn in the laundry, we had red bags, red bags, you had to turn them inside out as you put them in the washing machine and the clothes in there went onto a high wash due to them being covered in faeces or urine.

Pat and her team had already spent all morning purposefully putting the laundry that I had just cleaned straight back into the washing basket trolleys and were filling them up so high that I was struggling to keep up with the work load. Even though I knew that most of the clothes were clean I had to re-clean them due to them becoming cross contaminated with the dirty clothes.

I placed a red bag into the washing machine, locked the door and turned it on. I had my back to the machine and was ironing some light brown trousers, my mind was elsewhere as I was in fear of what was going to happen next when I heard clunk, clunk, eeek clunk clunk.

"What the...?" I thought to myself as I spun around and looked towards were the noise was coming from.

Horrified at what I was visually met with I shot forward and wacked the emergency stop button on the washing machine.

As it ground to a halt I inspected the large scissors through the glass, they were sticking through £75 pounds worth of Men's trousers, they had sliced a massive slit down the trouser leg to the bottom of the pants.

As I opened the machine I also realised that a butterfly needle had been purposely placed in there along with a urine soaked pad hidden in some knickers which had then been wrapped in female trousers.

The care staff wanted to get to me, and they were.

About 2 days later I was with my manager and she was concerned and confused as to why she could not remove a smell in which was coming out of one of the resident's room. The room had been deep cleaned and there was still a strong smell of faeces emulating from the room. Eventually she found the smell, a pad full of human shit had been placed in between the mattress and the bed slats right in the centre of the bed. The only way in which this could have been achieved is if one person held or removed the mattress and the other place the pad there. This had been clearly done purposely.

As time went on and the weeks passed I started to become ill, even though I had not realised it at the time I had lost a lot of weight and was not eating properly. I was going to work angry and coming home angry. I was snappy with my wife and had not got much patience with my eldest daughter.

In the nursing home there was a man whom in which I was very fond of, he was in the middle room in the middle corridor out of the three. He was ex RAF and you could tell that back in his younger years that he was a force to be reckoned with. He was a short man but wide framed. Frail now and walked with a wheeled Zimmer frame.

I walked into the lounge area were Pat was sat on one of the high backed and wooden sided chairs, the ex-Military resident stood looking out of the window.

"Hey, joe" Pat says laughing as I walk into the room.

"Mr R**** (Name blocked out for confidentiality purposes) believes that he can see a lion in the field, don't you Mr R****!" Pat said laughing and pointing towards the outside grounds of the nursing home.

Ignoring Pat, I smiled at the resident and asked him if he was ok.

"I am lad, can you see that Lion?" he asked as he pointed to the far end of the garden out of the window.

"I can mate, it's cool that buddie." I said giving him a thumb up and leaving the room pretending that Pat was not there.

It was obvious that there was no lion there, but he could see it, and there was no way I was upsetting him by telling him otherwise, nor was I getting involved in Pats pathetic little games. Mr R**** had served in the military for our country, probably been shot at and Beaton up in his life time, and there she was, treating him like crap.

The straw that broke the camel's back was a situation with a lady whom was mentally able, she knew what was going on around her and she was quite a friendly and chatty little lady. Yet she had mobility issues, she could not take herself to the toilet and she could not walk without staff assistance.

I was in the main bathroom collecting a laundry bag full of washing when I heard her crying out.

"Help, help me, I need help now, followed by sobbing"

I knew exactly what it was that was wrong with her, she needed the toilet, even though the care staff at times were not that busy if she asked to go to the toilet more than once in a 2-hour period she would be left. This would inevitably result in her wetting herself and becoming upset and humiliated. This would also result in Pat shouting at her.

There was many a time I would remove myself from the corridor whilst wiping a tear from my eye, no matter what I did no one listened, no one cared. And those whom did care, and listen were in the same boat as me, If they did take a stand, they were viciously bullied and made to feel inadequate.

It got to a stage where you questioned yourself, you questioned your sanity. "Is this really happening?" "Am I wrong for pointing out that this is abuse, and should not be tolerated?"

It was about 1 week after this incident that I decided that I had had enough. I had had enough of going to work feeling sick with anxiety, I had had enough of hearing elderly women and men cry as they were ridiculed by the staff that were meant to be protecting them. I had had enough of being ignored, I was tired, I was poorly, and I did not know what to do to stop the abuse nor whom to contact.

I walked into the manager's office at 10am on the morning that I decided to leave. I was 3 hours late for the shift, I had my work clothes in my hand and my notice. My notice read that I was terminating my employment with immediate effect due to inadequate response regarding the issues around safeguarding.

I stopped at the office door and waited for the manager to look up from her mobile phone, "Give me a second whilst I send this txt" she said glancing at myself then looking back at her phone seemingly disinterested. I waited patiently and silently as I watched her long fingers scurry from button to button at speed. I felt the knot in my stomach tighten as I

waited, and waited. I was stood here with my clothes and my notice and she evidently gave no fucks.

Eventually she looked up from her phone before placing it on the desk in front of her.

"How can I help you?"

She asked gesturing for me to sit down.

As I sat across from her I looked directly at her and into her eyes. She was a good-looking woman, I would say in her late 40s, she had a seemingly caring nature, almost motherly, but she was somewhat naïve and had seemingly no leadership qualities, I almost felt sorry for her as I sat looking at her.

"I have worked here for 8 months, and in that 8 months I have seen some of the most horrific abuse I have ever seen" As I was talking I could feel my voice start to shake and heart beat begin to rise as my temper began to creep in.

"And I have reported this on numerous occasions, and nothing has been done, so I am leaving, I have had enough." At this point my voice had become slightly louder than I had intended, and Helen had stopped smiling and was now glowering at myself like you would a naughty child.

"Right, well let me stop you there" she replied.

"Things have been escalated but these things take time..."

"How much time?" I cut her up. "People are being abused whilst these things are taking time!" I said standing up, annoyed.

"What would need to change for you to come back?" She asked suddenly mellow again and leaning back in her seat.

"Get new care staff, and I would consider it"

And at that I walked out, never to return.

In addition to this part of the book, it must be noted that I have since reported everything to an external safeguarding agency, due to my realising the seriousness of the abuse which had taken place whilst I was reliving the situation by writing it. So, upon receipt of this book I am hoping one of two things would have happened.

If the safe guarding has not dealt with it sufficiently then I will be going to the police. If this does not work, then I will be naming and shaming the nursing home on my social media and asking for people to come forward from that time and from the last 6 years through which I have not been there.

Hopefully allowing for the care staff that still work there to be removed from their posts, one of them that abused I know for a fact being a manager there present day.

I did not know back then that there was access to external safeguarding, if I knew back then what I know now, I would have acted sooner.

Chapter 16.

Getting thrown out.

Whilst all of this was happening at the nursing home I still had home life to contend with. At the time one child that needed love and support, and my wife, whom going through a rough patch herself needed as much support as I could provide her with.

I had been home from work for no longer than an hour when we received a knock on the door, one which sounded stern, like that a police man would have. I answered gingerly, feeling guilty even though I knew I had not done anything illegal. It was my landlady, Lela.

Me and Sophie looked at each other gingerly as she walked into the dining area. It was not like her to come with no warning, and we did not know where the cat was, the cat we were not meant to have.

She asked if she could sit down. As she sat she fumbled nervously with her fingers. Her dark brown scarf loosely draped around her neck.

"I am getting Married, err, so I need to sell the house"

As the words came out of her mouth, the last part of the sentence rushed, she clenched her hands anxiously, she had a soft voice, but it shook as she spoke this time. As I looked at her and smiled I wondered how long she had been plucking

up the courage to come and tell us? How many times had she rehearsed this conversation?

I thought back to the newspaper article myself and Sophie had found folded in that peculiar way on the kitchen table. Had it been a sign? The glass throwing itself against the back door, was that a sign as well? A get out sign? It certainly seemed that way to me.

Because of the visit myself and my wife ended up moving into this wonderful 3 bedroomed house that was semi-detached with a garage. It was beautiful……In a great location and with a nice garden…. But as we soon found out, it came with problems, massive problems.

The first problem was the psychotic next-door neighbour. Harsh, but in this instance true.

The problems with her started the first summer that we were living there.

My grandparents at the time had come to visit us. It was a summers evening and my children were upstairs playing in their room, my grandparents sat in our living room.

I jumped up startled upon hearing the loud, "Bang, Bang, Bang" on the door.

"Who the hell is that?" I said to Sophie as I walked towards the front door, a little startled, half expecting to see a police man, or worse, a debt collector.

A large figure loomed in the doorway.

I hesitated a second, took a deep breath in and then opened the door.

"Who in the hell, is that car! Get it moved!" The women shrieked pointing her fat finger in my face and showering me in spit. Her long greasy blonde hair bobbing about on her fat bulbous head.

I just stood there for a second, took a back and slightly confused as to why there was a large fat angry woman screaming at me about a car that was parked on my own driveway. I studied her. The flab on her stomach rolled over the top of her tight-fitting jeans, she had 3 fat rolls that seemed to congeal into one another that stopped just underneath her gigantic boobs. Her neck looked like it was ready to eat a child, and her head was huge. In addition to this she was angry.

"Just hang on a minute" I said holding my hand up in front of myself as if to shush her as I stepped onto the door mat out of my doorway.

"What are you on about? My car is on my drive what are you talking about?" I asked now standing in front of her.

"Here you idiot, here look! The wheel is touching a blade of grass!"

Walking over to where the furious fat women was stood, whom by now was red in the face and showering everything in spit as she spoke, I looked down at the spot at where she was pointing and began to laugh.

Where the car was parked was on my driveway, there was 1 blade of her grass touching the underside of the rubber tyre that was half on and half off my driveway the weight of the car on my drive.

"Are you kidding me?" I asked her slightly annoyed yet at the same time amused at her rage over a blade of grass.

"Get it moved!" she snarled pointing her car key in my face and screwing her face up in anger.

"Whatever, you silly women." I said as I turned to walk away.

I suddenly broke into a backwards run as she walked towards me her fists clenched and down by her side.

"You what!" she thundered as she began to run at me, her car keys clasped tightly in her hand somewhat like the way you would hold a knife. As she thundered towards me I suddenly realised that her intention was to stab me, turning around I ran. She was armed and a lot bigger then myself. As I jumped the step leading up to my front door, I slammed it firmly shut in her face as she tried to barge through it I put my foot behind it, locking it from inside.

That was the first time we met the neighbour's.

This lady was somewhat relentless, she was not just relentless, but she was a complete nutter, and dangerous to, she did not care whom it was that had parked or gone near her grass, she would come out and verbally and or physically attack them.

When we first moved into the property Sophie was heavily pregnant with my youngest daughter. It was a few weeks after we had moved in when we met our psychotic neighbour for a second time.

My eldest child had got out of the car and stood on the grass that ran up the side of our driveway, making it nearly impossible not to stand on it when exiting the vehicle.

I was walking into the house with my then heavily pregnant wife and my eldest daughter when I heard the women shout something to us about her grass.

Ignoring her we went inside the house and closed the door. A few seconds later there was a loud banging, I ignored it at first, but the banging got louder and louder to the point that it was starting to scare the little one.

"What do you want!" I asked opening the door and standing with my arms folded in the doorway. I had had enough and there was no need for this behaviour.

"Your daughter stood on my grass!!"

"And?" I replied opening my arms.

"What do you want me to do about it? Its grass?"

"IT'S MY GRASS!!" she shouted, this time waving the sharp end of her car key in my face and stepping forward as if trying to get into my house.

Hearing the commotion my wife appeared and stood to the right side of me, heavily pregnant.

"Listen, stop being a silly woman and go away before I call the police" she said calmly.

"You what! What did you just call me?" The lady snarled as she clenched her fists tightly and shoved myself backwards making me stagger into my hall way, shooting forward past me she swung her arm in an upward stabbing motion towards Sophie s clearly pregnant stomach with her car keys clenched tightly in her fist.

Regaining my balance, I swung down with my right arm and blocked the potentially fatal blow, stepping in front of Sophie I pushed the women backwards and shouted at her to get off my driveway before slamming the door in her face and locking it.

As well as the neighbour trying to kill myself and my wife and at one point my unborn daughter, throughout the 2 years that we lived in the property, we had another problem that was also posing a large threat.

The garage that was attached to the side of the house in which we were living had begun to sink and lean to one side. There was a long thin crack up the gable end of the building from the top to the bottom, which also proceeded straight through the middle of my daughter's bedroom. From inside her room the plasterboard had also begun to crack and separate. In addition to this the tiles in the bathroom had started to crack around the bath and the bath had started to move away from the wall.

This was clearly a concern for my family and myself as we were paying a good amount of money to live there and the house had become unsafe to live.

The situation I reported to my landlord, on several occasions during about 3 months but nothing was done, in fact they seemed somewhat disinterested in my complaints and eventually sent us a letter, giving us a month to leave.

During the time we had been living in the house with the dodgy garage I had left the nursing home and created my cleaning business as a small business venture, and as a method of creating an income. One of the people that I met through the business lived in a posh town in a very large house. She had us cleaning for her for 2 years and we became somewhat close. She was one of our very first customers.

Her name was Linda, I remember the first time in which we met as if it was yesterday. I watched my fuel gauge intently as I drove from the town off Macclesfield to Prestbury. The fuel gauge was below the red line and I had no money left at all. But I had to get to this woman's house as I had to take her on as a customer. We only had 2 customers so far and they were putting food on the table, just.

It was winter, and it was cold and slippery as I pulled into her driveway, the driveway was tilted downwards towards the house, so I placed my foot on the footbrake and pulled up the handbrake as I came to a halt. Stepping out of the vehicle I was careful as I placed my foot on the floor, it was icy, and I didn't want to slip. I breathed in deeply as I walked up to the front door. It was clear that they had money, serious amounts of money.

The house sat proudly below the driveway. The house was massive, it had a double garage that was attached to the side of it. The house itself stone in structure.

I breathed in deeply as I walked towards the front door, for some reason I was nervous, I was never nervous meeting customers normally so why now?

It was a few seconds after knocking when the solid blue front door opened. Behind it stood a woman, she was in her late 40s, but she looked a lot older than that.

As I followed her into the building I realised just how grand and posh the house was. I looked up as I walked through the door, the staircase ran up the right-hand wall next to the entrance to a study. It had a silver hand rail and frame which housed thick glass that acted as the banister rails. The stairs themselves thick cream carpet with thin red and black lines crossing each other in a square shape. The floor beneath my feet near the front door was white stone, textured beneath my socks with white grouting in-between each tile.

As I entered the kitchen I offered a hand to the rather large and tall fellow stood near the kitchen table.

"Joe from team mean clean, nice to meet you" I smiled as I shook his hand.

I was nervous as I glanced around the kitchen, Granite worktops sat proudly on their dark brown wooden cupboards. The large American style stainless steel fridge freezer and ice machine stood in the corner of the room. The house shouted wealth. I had never been nervous at a customer's house, so I was struggling to understand as to why I was nervous now.

As I drove home I mulled over the conversation in my head. Linda had signed the contract, every two weeks she was to have a clean. I was not to go upstairs, and I was only to clean the ground floor. The hours and finances discussed and agreed upon. Her and her husband had seemed friendly enough, Yet I felt uneasy. Nervous. Was it the size of the house? Was it because she was posh? Or was it because they reminded me of Mark and his wife. I could not place my finger on it.

It took 6 months into working for Linda when I started to become comfortable, relaxed even. She began to tell me more and more about herself. Where she was bought up, her struggles throughout life and her heartaches. In return I did the same. Told her about myself, let her in.

It got to the stage that I would look forward to going to her house, even though we would get into long winded conversations id work hard and clean as she was the kind of person that had to have everything perfect.

It was 1 year and a half into working for this lady when we became close. She had asked me about my parents, told me that they should be proud of me as I was such a hard worker and such an honest and reliable person. As I was listening to her I felt myself choke up. I wiped a tear from my eye as I squeezed the toilet duck into her downstairs toilet. Forcing a smile as not to cry I turned to where she was stood and then looked down at the box to where my cleaning things where stored. Placing the toilet duck into the box I grabbed the polish and starting to clean the large wooden chest that was situated below the staircase.

"So,......Do you see much of your parents?" Linda asked, seemingly irritated at the fact that I had not elaborated on her comment.

"My mum is dead, she was murdered" I explained calmly as I continued to gently move her pottery from one place to the other as I cleaned underneath it.

"Just got to mop, then I am done" I said cheerfully an hour later. She had spent most of the time that I was there talking to me and following myself around the house. We had talked about my mum, my dad and the time I spent in foster care. Handing me cash and giving myself a hug I left her house. I had started to feel like I belonged somewhere, like there was a mother figure in my life, a mother figure through which I had always desired. There is no one that could ever replace my actual mum, my biological one, but having one as a fill in gap, I was sure that she would not mind.

6 months after this conversation I was facing being homeless, my whole family was facing homelessness. The private rented properties wanted too much money, money we did not have at the time yet were trying to find, and the council had no housing for ourselves, we were on a list, a never-ending list.

I was back at Linda s house cleaning her living room when I asked for her to do me a character reference, we had fallen out with the landlady that we were currently with due to the situation with the garage so there was no hope of getting a decent reference from her.

"Yea sure, what for?" she asked seemingly concerned.

After explaining the situation Linda disappeared into her

kitchen for ten minutes or so, she then returned and gestured for me to follow her.

"Listen" she whispered not wanting the decorator in the conservatory area to hear what she was saying.

"I am in a financial position to buy you a house, we will by it and you rent it out, I will do it for you, as a mother figure."

I just stood there for a second staring at her open mouthed, this woman was willing to by my family a house, and she wanted me to effectively be her "Son".

Chocked up I did not know what to say, so I just threw my arms around her instead and thanked her. I wanted a mother figure, I wanted somewhere for my family to live that would be safe. As I finished the clean at Linda s house I felt somewhat joy and happiness.

But for some reason there was something niggling at me, my gut instinct was telling me not to trust this woman, not to go ahead with moving into one of her houses and not to trust her. I ignored it.

Chapter 17.

Flashback.

One early morning, I got into my car and drove down to the hanger which I used to clean. It was 3 am in the morning and it was cold and dark. I felt weird as I was driving towards the building, it felt as if someone was watching me and I kept turning around in my seat to see if there was anything there, but there was nothing, just an empty seat and darkness.

As I unloaded the car and entered the Hanger, I felt unsafe as if I was going to be attacked, I shut the door quickly behind me as I fumbled with the keys to lock it.

Calming myself down I walked through the large yellow doorway and into the Large metal hanger, the roller shutter door directly opposite me rattled in the wind as I looked around. It was empty, yet I still felt as if I was being watched.

Taking a right into the kitchen I made my way over to the dishwasher, as I started to load it I kept glancing over at the door that was now on my right-hand side, parallel to where the dishwasher was situated. I expected someone to be stood looking through the small pain of glass in the door, but no one was there.

As I finished cleaning the kitchen I was sure that someone was there with me, I was certain that I was being watched.

Making my way into the Men's toilets I glanced around the hanger as I pushed open the large blue door, it was ice cold, I felt the hair on the back of my neck stand on end, I was frightened as the door closed behind me.

I tried to block out the relentless thought that someone was watching me. As I wiped the sink with the blue cloth I felt someone step behind me. I breathed in shallowly as I felt their breath on the back of my neck, I then spun on my heel, expecting to be greeted with a robber.

What I was greeted with was much worse, staring back at me was a woman with black hair, matted to her forehead with blood, her eyes dark and sunken into her skull and her facial features twisted and distorted. She was wearing a white nightgown, it came down to her knees, her legs so painfully thin you could see bone. As I scanned the nightgown I realised that it had 2 dark red blood stains around the chest area, created by 2 stab wounds. There was blood sprayed around the bottom of the gown itself. In shock, I stepped back and into the sink. As my heart pounded hard in my chest I closed my eyes, the women, she was my mum.

"She is not real, she is not real" I told myself over and over. I wanted to scream, I wanted to run but I did neither, I was frozen to the spot. Tears ran down my cheeks as I opened my eyes, she was gone. I was terrified, yet at the same time I knew she was not real, I knew she was my mum.

As I cleaned the toilets I had to keep wiping the tears away from my eyes, stopping what I was doing every so often as I was sobbing so hard.

"For fucks sake! Pull yourself together man!" I scolded myself as I forced myself to continue with the job.

Walking toward the men's toilet door to exit I stopped again, feeling the presence of someone there, behind me, this time the feeling intensified as I stood frozen to the spot.

I breathed in deeply, I was terrified, but I forced myself to turn around. As I turned, slowly this time, I was greeted again with my mum, she was the same as before but the stab wounds on her chest were more prominent. They were open and deep, deep enough that I could see deep into her chest.

"Mum…" I said through sobs as I reached out my hand, my vision was by now blurred with tears, so I wiped my eyes with the sleeve of my t shirt, temporarily looking away, looking back, she was gone.

It was getting to 6am in the morning and I was still upset, I knew that at 6:30 the office workers started to arrive, and I did not want them to see me crying, especially the women, so I loaded my car and locked up the offices and armed it.

As I was driving away in my 4wd I looked in the rear-view mirror, staring back at me was my mum, as before her hair matted with blood and her eyes sunken and dark. I slammed on the brakes, skidding to a halt, I got out of the vehicle, I was standing in the middle of the main road, my car stopped blocking both lanes, but I did not care, I held my head in my hands and shouted for her to get out of my head.

Eventually I got home, ashamed, I was ashamed of myself for crying, I should be tough, strong and invincible, the man of the house. Yet here I was, crying into my wife s shoulder after my mind had created these images, these horrific images.

The next day I was at home with Sophie, it was Saturday night, I was washing the pots at the sink and Sophie was drying them.

I felt faint and a bit sick as I washed the large carving knife under the tap, I stepped backwards and stared at Sophie wide eyed. I watched myself as I plunged the large knife into her chest and stomach area, again and again I stabbed her, the blade cutting through her flesh easily and effortlessly, until she dropped to her knees, before falling backwards onto the wooden floor and lying there lifeless, it was strange but there was no sound, this was happening but there was no sound. Looking down at the knife I watched as the thick red blood oozed down the handle from the tip of the blade and onto my hand. I threw the knife in the sink and backed into the corner of the room my mouth opened wide, what the fuck have I done.

"Joe? Hello, Joe? Are you ok?" Suddenly I hear Sophie s voice, she is stood directly in front of me, her hand on the side of my face.

I looked down at my hands, then on the floor, then at the sink. There was no blood, my wife was ok, relief flooded my body as I stood and stared at Sophie, a confused expression on my face.

"I need help" I muttered as I stood staring at her.

Chapter 18.

Hypnotherapy.

It was the following week when I found myself contacting a local hypnotherapist, I had tried to find a face to face counsellor. But they were too expensive at the time, so hypnotherapy was the next best thing. In addition, he was walking distance from where I was living at the time. I felt a mixture of shame and anger at having to ring a professional to help me with my issues. At the same time however, I was looking forward to getting the problems resolved, not for me, for the sake of my children and my wife. What I was experiencing was horrific, what I was seeing was beyond comprehension and I was terrified that I was physically going to do someone harm.

My heart thumped hard in my chest as I entered the carpet shop. It was getting late at night as I closed the wooden door behind me, looking to my left there was a locked room, a sign on it, please do not disturb, hypnotherapy in progress. Looking across the room, throughout the mounds of carpet rolls there was a short fat man stood near a large industrial printer with glasses on. He gave me a wave and shouted for me to give him five minutes then he would be with me.

"No worries" I replied.

A few minutes later I was entering the locked room with the short fat man by my side, he was a jolly little fellow. In front of me was a large brown cushioned chair and to the right was a poster, it was bright blue in colour and read the words. "Freedom through hypnosis"

Sitting across from the man in the large chair I tried to relax but I felt somewhat anxious as to what was going to happen.

I tried to explain to the therapist the reason that I was here, but he did not want to know. He cut me off mid-sentence, explaining to me that I would tell him during my hypnotherapy.

Sitting in the chair I breathed in and out deeply as I tried to relax. It took a while but after a few minutes I was calm, and my breathing was steady.

Closing my eyes, I listened to the man's voice.

It was somewhat calming and reassuring with the hypnotic music playing in the background.

As I listened a field appeared in front of me, I was in my own mind, like when Neo enters the matrix, his physical body staying in one place yet his mind and physical body also experiencing another dimension, suddenly no longer was I in the small room but I was in a field. Staring at a small river, the water in the river was clear and fresh, it was running steadily, as I looked at it I had an urge to jump in and play in it, the river seemed to be inviting me into its current.

My attention suddenly shifted and looking up I saw a bridge directly in front of me, it was made from solid oak, it was yellow in colour, strong and sturdy, I found myself stepping onto the large oak bridge and standing in the middle of it. The sky had turned somewhat cloudy as I looked up and the sun had gone in leaving a slight chill against my skin.

I realised that I was carrying a rucksack and I found myself taking it off my back and placing it onto the floor, it was heavy, very heavy.

As the rucksack hit the wooden bridge I realised that it was suddenly empty.

"Look to your left-hand side, you will notice some things, you need to put them into the rucksack."

I looked up towards the sky, the cool breeze seemed to seep through my body as I look down at my left hand. Below it a pile of things that needed to be thrown away.

I reached down and clasped my hand around the jagged knife that was covered in dark red blood, I felt sick and slightly faint as I picked it up and dropped it into the bag, the blood slippery between my fingers, next I picked up a big clumpy doll, it was large and lumber some, A thick tuff of ginger hair on its head, I knew who it was. That I threw into the bag with force, with anger. More and more things appeared, a brown teddy, not a normal teddy bear, an animal, a weasel, well used, my dad had bought it me from prison. If only I understood why he was in there when I was snuggling up to it at night. I didn't understand, I just wanted my dad.

"Once you have filled the bag, I want you to throw it over the edge of the bridge and into the river."

Snapping out of the anger that I was feeling I did as I was instructed. Picking up the bag with great difficulty as it was so heavy I managed to sit it on the hand rail, holding it there for a second I got my breath then pushed it over the edge, it made a loud splash as it landed in the river before I watched it float off into the distance.

"Now you have done that, you will notice that in front of you there is a pathway. I want you to cross the bridge and walk along the path telling me what you see."

As I looked in front of me a forest appeared out of no-were, stepping off the bridge I stepped onto the pathway, it was a mustard coloured pathway and It was made of gravel. As I walked the gravel crunched beneath my feet, the trees provided shade from the sun that had now started to beat down hard. As I studied my surroundings I noticed that all was not as it seemed. The branches of the trees were gnarled and twisted and some of them looked like hands trying to reach out and drag me into the dense forest. Looking down at my feet then to the left I noticed that the grass verges had become somewhat thicker, brambles and nettles were also entwined within the thick grass and weaved in and out of each other as if protecting and hiding a terrible secret below them.

As I walk further into the forest I notice that the light is blocked out even more so by the trees and it has gone somewhat darker, opening my arms and feeling a pang of excitement, I hold my wife as she appears in front of me out of no were, releasing my grip on her she stands by the side of me.

My 2 daughters come running towards me and Sophie from behind the trees, excitement and relief flows through my body as they run towards me, me and Sophie now both kneeling with our arms open wide.

I gasp sharply and stand up, hugging myself as the wind seeps through my body I look around concerned, I am alone, and the atmosphere has become intimidating.

"I am alone"

I explain to my therapist as I look around the cold and uninviting forest, everything seeming scarier and more intense by the second.

"It is ok joe, keep walking, it is ok, tell me what you see"

The voice again coming out of no were, it calms me as I continue to walk down the gravel pathway, the forest is intimidating and scary, yet I feel assured that what I am doing is right.

I walk for a while through the forest, the therapist asking me every now and again if I can see anything new.

After a while I stop abruptly and turn to my right-hand side. Out of nowhere a terraced building has appeared, it is slightly hidden behind 2 trees. Walking towards it I scan the front of the house. I step onto the dark grey tarmac footpath and walk to the dark brown fence. Placing my hand on the fence I study the garden. It is messy, severely overgrown and clearly not cared for, the fence itself is damaged badly, barely serving its purpose as a fence.

"I know this garden, I am scared" I tell my therapist as I stand looking into the garden, my hand on the fence.

"It's ok Joe, can you enter the garden or the house joe?" The therapist askes calmly.

"Yes"

I reply as I flip up the metal catch and walk through the gate which wobbles under the weight of my hand, I shut the gate gently as it is very wobbly and there is a smell emitting from the rotten wood. As the gate clicks shut I turn and force myself to walk forward one step at a time, I take my time as I navigate the cracked and disintegrating walkway, getting closer and closer to the large brown wooden door.

When I reach the door, I notice that like the garden fence and gate it is rotten and disintegrated, the top glass panel in the door has been smashed and there are jagged shards of glass left in the door.

Reaching out with my hand I push it gently; the uneven and peeling paint work feels rough under my fingers. The door makes a creaking sound as I push it exposing a dark and dingy room. Stepping into the room I feel my insides twist and turn with a mix of part fear and part disgust. The room is scattered with partially open bin bags that seem to crawl up the wall, an outdated television set sits in the corner of the living room on top of a brown cabernet…. the atmosphere in the house is present with a severe tension that you could slice through with a knife.

Slightly panicked I suddenly realise that I am no longer alone, there is someone else in the house. Turning away from the sickening scene of the living room I turn towards were the noise is coming from. The smell of cigarette smoke overpowers the area in the corridor as I walk towards the kitchen, glancing at the walls and the ceiling I run my hand along one of the walls, it is stained brown with cigarette tar.

I enter the kitchen; the door is open and as I walk in I turn my head to the right. There is a large brown dining table which is dirty, the top of the table seems to be covered in a thick grease, it does not look like it has been wiped down for a long time. I then pan the room, from the dirty dining table I spot a picture on the wall, the picture features a gold frame around it and inside it there is a field like background and there looks to be a soldier with a red jacket on in the forefront, but it is blurred.

Suddenly I freeze on the spot, I can see my dad, a lean yet powerful figure, he is stood over my mum, shouting at her and hitting her.

"I can't move" I explain to the therapist panicked.

"It is ok to just stand their Joe" he replies calmly and reassuringly.

I stand there frozen, unable to move my body at all, Fear engulfs my body as I watch my dad raise his hand above his head for a 3rd time.

"How old are you Joe?" my therapist questions after a few seconds of silence, prompting me to look down at my child like hands.

"4" I respond now tearful.

"Can you move now?" He says calmly completely un-phased by the fact that I am now crying.

"I am trying to, but I can't" as I stand staring at my dad I try to move my hand, my arm or my feet, nothing moves, I am stuck to the spot, panicked.

"I can't, I am to scared, I can't, I am scared." I repeat becoming distressed tears running down my face.

"Can big Joe help little Joe?"

Upon hearing this suggestion, I hear the front door to the house open, A lean yet powerful figure walks towards me. I feel secure and safe as Joe s large powerful hand firmly but gently grips my hand and gestures for me to leave the building with him. Feeling safe and secure I turn and walk through the already open door. As we exit the building we both work together to push the door shut, pushing down hard into the floor our shoes grip the concrete tightly and we slam the door shut with as much force as we can muster.

As we both turn to leave we must use every muscle in our body to keep walking forwards, leaning forwards we walk down the pathway and back through the wooden gate, onto the gravel in the wood, its hard work to keep walking forward as it feels like there is an invisible force pulling us back to the house, but we fight it. Leaving mum in that situation is almost unbearable but what could we do? We were too scared to stay and protect her.

"I am alone, little Joe has now gone"

I tell my therapist as I walk down the pathway, I am now walking freely. The trees loom overhead as the weather suddenly changes, there is a storm coming.

A large stone building appears in front of me, it has a large solid wooden door. As I move closer to the building the size of it overwhelms me. As I scan my surroundings I notice that I am stood on one of the very few visible parts of the path outside of the building. The rest of the path is overgrown, entangled with weeds and thick grass.

I stop for a second as I get to the large wooden door, the rusty handle in the centre of the door has got my attention. I inspect it for a second, running my finger over the rust I watch as it drops onto the weeds below.

I slip through the door as it is partially open, The temptation to powerful not to. As I get into the building the darkness engulfs my body, the only light coming in the room through the gap in the door behind me, casting a thin stream of light upon the concrete floor.

I walk forwards confidently; my body feels like it has been taken over and is being driven by an unknown source. Strip lights begin to appear on either side of the ceiling parallel to one another, lighting the decent down the tunnel that has now become steep and increasingly tight in width. Stopping abruptly, I turn to my left, then my right, then back again. I stay there for a moment, I am stood in a four-way junction, each corridor lit by bright strip lights, yet each corridor going down to a different destination. Suddenly I have the urge to follow the corridor on my right, as if someone is pulling at my arm to do so.

  Turning to the right I begin to walk up the steep ascent that has appeared, the walk uphill is hard work and the concrete beneath my feet becomes slightly unstable as I walk forward one step at a time, each one becoming more and more difficult than the other. Just before I am about to stop walking the path evens out and it becomes easier on my legs. As I walk my mood shifts and I suddenly start to feel light in my body. I notice a light at the end of the tunnel and I break into a steady jog. As I exit the weird tunnel I feel the sun beating down on me, slowing until I stop I look up at the clear blue sky, not a cloud in sight.

  Looking back down again I notice that there is in front of me a different country. It is France, excitement grows in my body as I break into a run. I need to get there, I need to see my uncle. Suddenly I lock out both of my legs and skid to a halt on the gravel. In front of me a large hole has just opened, stopping me from getting into the country.

A deep feeling of sadness seems to engulf my body as I wonder to the grass verge near the pathway that has now appeared.

Sitting down I hold my head in my hands, I do not want to move nor, do I want to do anything, I do not want to be here.

Suddenly I feel the ground beneath me vibrating, jumping up I run, the ground from underneath me is disappearing. As my foot leaves the grass the ground beneath it falls away, at this point I am now running for my life.

In the distance, I see a large rock, I do not know why but I do know that the rock is safe, I stretch my arms and legs out as far as they can go as I leap towards the rock, I land in the centre of it surprised at how soft the rock is. As I watch the ground around the rock disappears I sit there calmly, I feel safe, this is my rock.

"When you are ready you need to get back onto the path and walk towards the bridge"

I had not realised that I had been giving my therapist a running commentary on the situation at hand, either that or he could read my mind.

I climbed off the rock and onto the solid gravel pathway that had suddenly appeared. As I walked back towards the bridge I made sure that I stayed in the middle of the pathway as all the land on each side of it was none existent, there was just blackness presuming thousands of feet drop if I was to step off the edge.

As I reach the bridge I die a little inside.

"The bag is back" I tell my therapist.

Chapter 19.

Facing my deepest fears.

Buried, that is what I realised as I made my way back towards the therapist's office two weeks following the first visit. I felt hurt and angry that my past had been hidden from me and my biological mum and dad had never been openly discussed. Every-time I had tried to discuss my past I had been shut down.

"When you are 18, when you are 21 we will discuss it" were the excuses.

I remember telling Marks wife that I wanted to go and visit my biological mums grave.

"Bit morbid that, don't you think Joseph" was the reply.

I itched my nose as I continued the descent down the road to the therapist s office, something I always did when I was beginning to get agitated. Mark and his wife were morons who had lied and manipulated me for years for their own fucking gain. Pissed, that I was.

10/08/13 was the date my watch read as I stepped up onto the stone step and in through the front door of the carpet shop.

The short fat hypnotherapist greeted me with a smile and gestured for me to sit down in the large leather chair.

"Sit back, relax and close your eyes" the hypnotherapist instructs calmly.

"You are going to go deeper into your mind then you have ever been."

I look around as the gentle breeze makes the grass tilt slightly as it blows. The sun is out but there is a chill in the air. The river this time is running a little slower than before and the bridge looks slightly different, it is stable but the wood that holds the structure together is slightly thinner than the first time I walked across it.

As I reached the other side I stop and look at the path, I stand watching it intently as the ground in front of me falls away and stone steps appear leading into a deep hole in the ground. I walked down the stairs slowly, the steps hard beneath my feet, I hear a splash as I step in a small puddle that has formed in a hollow in one of the well-worn stones.

Stopping at the bottom of the stairway I study the door directly in front of me. It is painted blue and is solid in structure, the paint smelt fresh as I reached out to open it.

As my feet hit the floor I look down at them, realising that the floor is blue in colour with a mock-led effect and it is shiny, sterile and highly polished. I am in a hospital, I thought to myself as I stopped walking and scanned the room. I realise that I am in a hospital corridor. Doors adjacent to each other on either side of where I am stood. As I stand there they start to move, slowly at first but after a few seconds they move at high speed, as if on a conveyer belt going passed me in a forward's motion on the right-hand side but then coming back passed me in a backwards motion on the left.

Abruptly the doors come to a standstill, I realise that there is just a blank wall on the right, but the left wall is where the doors have settled. I walk slowly up the corridor until I feel the need to stop, stopping I turn my head to the left, followed by my body as I spin on the balls of my feet. The paint again smells fresh as if it's just been painted, I ponder for a second as I run my fingers over the silver numbers that have been carefully screwed to the top part of the door. The 1 and the 0-sitting side by side, Gently I depress the silver handle and push on the door exposing the hospital ward.

As I slowly walk down the centre of the ward I notice that there are 4 beds, 2 on either side, all the navy-blue hospital curtains pulled back exposing the empty beds, clear fresh white sheets neatly made on each bed almost inviting you to jump in and snuggle down.

Stopping I look at the bed on the far left of the ward, the covers pulled back as if someone has just climbed out of it, fresh flowers are in a clear vase on the wooden bedside cabernet. As they fade in and out I notice that the ward is disappearing, keeping my eyes closed I realise that I am back in the therapist's office.

"Keep calm and concentrate" he instructs firmly.

Suddenly I find myself back in the hospital, the flowers in the vase now vibrant, red roses sit proudly on top of their stems.

Turning towards the bed I breath in sharply and step back. The women s head is facing down, staring at the bedsheet. Her long black hair is drooping over the front of her face completely covering it from my view.

I walk forward gingerly, yet curious. As I get to the foot of her bed she snaps her head up making the hair slide back behind her ears exposing her face. I stagger backwards into the curtain behind me. "Her face, its distorted" I say as a single tear runs down my cheek, there is fear and sadness in my voice, a lump now in my throat.

Steading myself I freeze on the spot and stare at my mum, her left cheek her bone is on show, the flesh around it peeled back and some of it flapped down by the side of her face. Her eyes are deep and sunken into her skull, both sockets swollen, a mixture of deep blue and black. The rest of her skin is not skin, its flesh, a deep red in colour and pitted.

"Mum" I say as I cover my mouth with my hand, tears now streaming down my face.

In response, she raises her arm and points at me, her fingers and hands painfully thin, her whole-body skin and bone clearly malnourished.

"You! It is you" she shouts angrily, her finger quivering with rage.

"You did it, it's you"

"She s shouting at me" I tell my therapist, my body now shaking as my crying turns to sobs.

"Who are you Joe? Are you, you?" I look down at my hands, they are large, huge in fact, I have big fat fingers and massive palms. On my feet are large brown shoes, shiny coming to a point at the end, I notice that I am tall. My whole body feels large and cumbersome, almost like a wrestler.

"I am my dad" I tell him softly, almost not daring to speak at all in fear of what might happen next.

"What is he feeling Joe? What is your dad feeling?"

"No, no, no" I shout as I pull back, my dad's body is flooded with hate, anger and disgust. I pull back as much as I can, all my strength used to try and stop my dad as his hands land into my mum s already pulp beaten face. She screams and holds her hands above her head to try and shield herself from the blows to her head and face. She is now on the floor against the wall, curled up in a ball on the floor. Again, I try to pull back, using all my strength to stop my dad from hitting

her. Staggering backwards I land on my back on the floor, my body becoming detached from my dad's, as if I had stepped out of his shell and into my own.

As I slide across the highly polished hospital floor on my back I tilt my head upwards just in time to see dad slap my mum across the back of her head with an open palm.

Staggering to my feet I stand up, for a second I just stand there and watch, frozen with fear, I watch as my dad takes a step back and swings his foot in a backwards motion ready to kick my mum whilst she lies on the floor in a ball. I look down at my hands, I am me, 25 years old, strong and powerful enough to intervene, strong enough to do something about the abuse, strong enough to stop the abuse.

Rage fills my body as I walk towards dad at pace, grabbing the collar of his blue shirt I drag him off his feet and throw him to the floor, mum still lay on the floor in the faecal position trying to protect herself. Thick and dark red blood seeps from a crack in dad s skull, he must have done that on impact as he hit the floor I think to myself as I watch it begin to surround his head and neck area. Bending forwards, I grab the front of his shirt with both of my hands and drag him to his feet, before ramming his lifeless body against the hospital wall and furiously ramming my fists into him, blindly I swing at his ribs, left, right, left, right. I can feel his ribs beneath my fists as each knuckle digs into them and breaks them on impact, the cracking of each rib satisfying my thirst for revenge, exhausted and breathing heavy I step back and watch as his body slides down the wall leaving a smear of blood.

I look towards were my mum was, she is no longer on the floor. Stepping back wards I breath in deeply and my legs collapse from under me as I fall to me knees. Tears streaming from my face I try to stand up, but I cannot move. The sickening image playing over and over in my mind.

In the corner of the room my mum is hanging from her neck by a rope, her head, it twists making a fleshy ripping sound as the skin peels and splits around her neck, her whole head then detaches itself from her neck before hitting the floor with a sickening thud, I try to stand up, I try to move but I can't, the image plays over and over in front of me.

"Ripping sound, thud, ripping sound, thud." I watch as it detaches itself and then lands on the floor, before seemingly resetting itself and following the same process again and again.

Eventually the invisible source holding me in place seems to release me, I manage to turn away from the sickening scene, as I stand up to turn to leave I wipe tears from my eyes that were making my vision blurry. I hear another sickening thud behind me as I walk towards the exit of the ward.

Freezing to the spot, I stare at the bed to my right, in it a huge dark figure, grey in colour, it has no eyes, ears or nose, it does however have razor sharp teeth and blood red lips. Long strands of saliva dribbles from the grinning mouth onto the floor as it slides off the edge of the bed towards me.

"Can you talk to it?"

"I can't, I am too scared, it wants to hurt me" I tell my therapist.

Slowly I back up towards the exit of the ward, my eyes fixated on the creature that is gliding towards me at a slow and steady pace. I twist my hand behind me at an awkward angle, my fingertips frantically trying to find the door handle. Gripping the cold metal handle tightly I shove the door open and walk backwards into the corridor, the creature still coming towards me. Gripping the edge of the wooden door with my hand I pull at it to shut the creature in, it won't move, gripping the door with both hands I pull at it with all my strength, nothing happen end's, it won't budge. I have no choice, I turn and run. I run blindly through the long corridor, frantically trying to find another room, somewhere I will be safe, somewhere I can get away. My legs feel like they want to give way as I run but I keep pushing, the creature's teeth snapping at my heels. A spray of saliva splatters my heel as I feel the teeth snap shut just millimetres away from my skin.

I can see a room coming up to my left, the door is open partially, just enough for me to fit in side-wards, I have one shot at this. I hear the creature snarl closely behind me as I drop onto my side and slide through the door, as I get into the ward a spin myself round so I am on all fours, I scramble to my feet and run at the door, slamming it shut and locking it, I slide down the door exhausted, I hear a snarl and a bang as the creature throws itself against the door, followed by a Yelp and then silence, the only noise in the room being my heavy breathing.

As my breathing returns to normal I scan the room, it is another ward, just like the other one. I scramble to my feet and run across the room, there is a woman hanging by her neck from a rope. The rope is blood stained and dirty, yet it is thin, quickly I work, gripping the rope with my left hand I wrap my arm around the women with my right arm and lift her, creating slackness in the rope, she is thin and feeble. As the rope slackens I gently place my fingers in-between the rope and the women s neck, working my way around her neck I loosen the rope until it is loose enough to be lifted over her head. Taking care not to catch any of the deep cuts and bruises on the women s face I carefully and methodically lift the rope over her head and gently lower her to the floor, she is slightly smaller than me, so I must bend a little.

I stand for a second and stare at the women whom is now stood in front of me, staring back at me. Her face is badly bruised and swollen. Her eyes sunken deep into her head, and on her right cheek a flap of skin is folded down exposing flesh below. As I scan the women I notice that she is wearing a thin white nightgown which is covered in blood and is ripped in the left corner. Her body is thin and feeble, almost anorexic.

I bend slightly as the women places her arms around me and holds me tightly, I break down as I hug the women back and bury my head into her shoulder, it is the first time in 20 years that I have seen or hugged my mum.

"She s hugging me" I explain through sobs.

"Can she talk?" the therapist asks calmly.

Suddenly she is gone, I look around frantically the ward empty, spinning around to my left I notice a bed with the covers pulled back and flowers on the bedside cabernet. In it my mum. As I approach I notice that she looks healthier and the marks on her face have begun to heal. I sit on the seat next to her and hold her hand, she is sat up in bed.

"She wants to talk but she can't." I explain to my therapist as she stares back at me, she opens her mouth, but no words come out.

I catch a glimpse of something across the room, it is my dad, he is back but he is behind the locked door, he cannot get in. The grinning idiot stares directly at me and my mum, I smile back, knowing he cannot get in and knowing that my mum is now safe.

I sit staring at my now healthy mum as a nurse in a white tunic approaches and stands at the end of the bed with a clipboard. The nurse starts to speak but I cannot hear what she is saying.

"I want to stay here forever" I think to myself as I grip tightly

onto mum s hand, she grips my hand back in response.

"You have to leave now." The therapist says calmly.

The words cutting through me like a knife I shout at him as the bed starts to fade.

Mums hand releases its grip and she starts to cry as she reaches out for me, both of her arms outstretched.

"I can't leave her" I shout as I try my best to grab at her outstretched arms.

Ignoring my pleas, the therapist talks fast,

"You need to come back out of the room, up the corridor, onto the gravel pathway and across the wooden bridge." His voice has an undeniable tone of panic in it as he tries to get me out of the trance like state.

I holdout my arms and shout "NOO" loudly as an invisible force seems to grip a tight hold of my waste and drags me backwards out of the room, up the corridor, onto the pathway and onto the wooden bridge.

I open my eyes, the last image in my mind being the wooden bridge. Looking up I cannot see the man in front of me, the tears in my eyes making him blurry.

"Just let it out" My therapist says calmly as I sob into a tissue.

Chapter 20.

Meeting my mum's murderer.

Before I went for therapy, when I was living in the haunted house in Macclesfield, which would have been in the year of either 2011 or 2012 I was learning and finding out about my biological family when I made the decision that I wanted to meet and talk to my dad, eh hem, sperm donor.

There were several reasons in which I wanted to meet my dad, one of the reasons was just that, I wanted a dad, and I had lots of burning questions, one of them, why did he kill my mum?

I remember my dad from when I was a child, apart from the bad stuff he did. Like remembering him giving my sister and brother the slipper, the reason unknown. And remembering standing at the window in his bedroom singing "rain, rain go away come back another day" thinking that it would make the rain go away, as dad was refusing to take my brother to karate if it did not stop raining.

Also remembering my brother crying as dad rammed him against a wall and twisted his arm up his back making him scream out in agony in front of myself, apart from all the bad things in which he did, eventually murdering my mum.

I wanted my dad. I wanted a dad.

There was few and far between, but there were occasions in which dad was nice to me. Such as when he used to say, "high five Joe, to slow." Whilst moving his hand away and laughing, before pinning me down and rubbing his stubble into my cheek, making me giggle and squirm under his weight.

And there was also one other time in which sticks with me, which was when we went fishing, it was a day in which I had a massive mixture of emotions. I remember Mum and Dad going for it on this day, more so dad. He was yelling at mum and waving his arms around in front of her, he then demanded that myself and my brother come outside with him, I remember following him and my brother out of the front door as he had requested, he slammed it shut as we walked outside, the door and frame straining under the impact.

The middle section is blank, but the next thing I remember is that I am sat on a fold down chair, my brother by the left of me, my dad in the middle of myself and my brother. Dad reaches down and picks a mealworm from the bucket, he then looks at me and smiles before piercing the side of the worm with the fishing hook. I watch as the hook enters the worm and comes out the other side, the worm wiggling frantically, stopping completely for a second and then frantically wiggling again. I wonder how much pain the worm must be in as I watch it wiggle, if it could scream it would be agonising screams.

Dad castes the fishing line, I wonder how mum is as I watch him fish. The water on the canal calm as the float bobs about gently on the water. For a few minutes all is silent, Dad is calm, and I feel safe, just for a moment.

"Pack it in!"

I hear my dad growl as he glowers at my brother.

"I fucking told you, you little shit!" Dad yells suddenly bursting into a fit of rage, I do not know if he was pushed, (more than likely) or if he fell but my brother then flipped backwards in his seat and rolled backwards onto the hard canal pathway, the seat landing on top of him.

I saw dad raise his hand above his head and then stop mid-air, as if he had suddenly realised that he was out in the open, not protected by the enclosed walls of our house. Beating your children and wife is frowned upon in public, but within closed doors, unless you tell someone, or they hear you scream, and have the brains to report it to the police, which is unlikely. Then beatings can go on for years with no-one any wiser. With my dad, everyone loved him, outside of the house he was the man.

"We are going home, fucking tidy up" dad snarled as he started to throw things into a metal box.

The memories of my dad are small, yet they are crystal clear in colour and vision. I remember dad back then, the way he looked, he was a stocky build, about 5 feet 5 and he was capable of being nice, when he wanted to, when he was going to gain something.

It was a Saturday morning, I was in my car after dropping Sophie off at work, on my way to the lay by in Congleton in which we had agreed to meet. As I had kissed her goodbye she had warned me to be careful and to prepare myself, be on my guard as she was worried. I was meeting a 1st degree convicted murderer, shit whom would not be worried.

As pulled up in the layby I turned off my car engine and gingerly stepped out of my vehicle, a blue ford escort. I slammed my door shut and locked it. As I approached the Honda civic brown in colour, a short bald fat man opened the driver's door and stepped out. I felt somewhat disappointed as he approached me, he was not the lean, yet stocky character in which I remember, he had no stubble and he walked slowly, with a crutch. Sunglasses covered his eyes, and the hand in which was not holding the crutch, was concealed in his pocket. He was wearing a brown jacket and blue jeans with white trainers.

"Long time dad" I said as I held out a hand to shake his, it was something in which I had been bought up to do, you meet someone you shake their hand, an ingrained habit, Dads hand was massive and was rough, as it engulfed mine I could not help but wonder if that was the hand that he had used to Ram the serrated knife into mums chest, his hands and arms were clearly powerful, he would not have had to use much force.

I pushed the thought out of my head for a second.

"Do you want to go to the pub? For a quiet drink and a chat?" Dad asked as he gestured for me to get into his car.

I hesitated for a second, "Its ok" he reassured me as I walked slowly to his vehicle. Stepping in the car I sat down in the passenger seat. Instantly my senses were overrun with the smell of cigar smoke. Sitting in the driver's side my sperm donor started to roll a cigar.

"Do you smoke?" He asked.

"No, I don't", I replied as he put the cigar into his mouth and proceeded to drive down the road towards a local pub.

As we pulled up outside the pub he told me about the work that he had been doing. Tree felling, working in a shop for a friend of his, and working in building.

I sat across from him outside the pub, he had bought me a coke, the first thing he had bought me as a parent in the last 17 years, before that it was the teddy he got for me from prison. I had watched him like a hawk as he took it from the bar tender and passed it to myself, as I drank it I was certain he had not laced it with anything, that was my concern, that he was going to lace my drink then do me in. I didn't talk much as we sat across from each other, he apologised that it had not worked out with Mark and his wife, and told me that he had a poorly finger, and that in the winter it ached. He explained that he had always thought of myself, especially in winter, because one day he was asleep on the sofa after a long day at work and I had come up to him and grabbed his finger making it crack, since then when it was cold he thought about me as his finger ached.

As we got back into the car I thought about the story that he had just told me, I believed him, maybe he did love me, maybe he did remember his children and maybe mum s murder was a big accident, maybe he had not meant to kill her.

As these thoughts raced through my mind dad noticed I was cold and turned the heating on in the car.

"Joe, I will do anything to get our relationship back"

"I have money, 20 thousand pounds saved, I also have friends, I can take you and your wife and children camping in a big static caravan, I will pay for it all" as these words left his mouth I felt sickened to my stomach, a little woozy and light headed as I looked at him, he had killed my mum in a caravan and was now offering to take me camping.

"Thank-you, I suppose" I muttered as I sat there, emotions were racing through my body, different emotions ripped through me like the wind from a storm unrooting trees.

"I will do anything" dad said as he turned to me.

"Why did you kill my mum?"

I asked, I suddenly felt dead inside, no anger, no love, no nothing, nothing other than disappointment and depression.

"It was you mum, and you, she wanted you, she was going on and on about how we had to get Joe out of care, she wanted me to just go and pick you up, but I couldn't. She was an alcoholic you know, drunk all the time, abusive towards me. Then one day I just picked up a knife and......" at that dad shrugged his shoulders and stopped talking.

As I got into my car I re ran the conversations over in my head. I felt uneasy, sick to my stomach.

"Bro I need to talk" I said as he answered the phone 1 week later. As I told him what happened he stopped me mid-sentence.

"Let me guess? His finger hurts in winter and it's because you pulled it, every time it is cold he thinks about you"

"How did you know he had said that bro?" I asked somewhat confused.

"Because he told me the exact same thing joe, but about me, how he remembered me in the winter, he is dangerous and a prolific liar and manipulator."

I felt sick, my gut was right, I had spent the last week ignoring dads calls and messages, I was confused and frightened as I putdown the phone to my brother.

As I listened to my phone ringing out I remembered what my brother had told me. If you shout at him down the phone he will put it down on you and pretend that he cannot hear you, he will then phone you back to try and throw you off track.

"Hello, I've been trying to get hold of you son"

"Dad, you lied to me" I said.

"You lied to me about mum, all I wanted was for you to tell the truth and you could not do that, I message you and you reply with one worded answers. Why dad, why can you not be honest, you disappoint me.........." At this point I was shouting as I gripped the wooden banister rail with my free hand and pulled at it trying to release some of my anger.

"Son, I can't read or write well, that is why my text messages are short and it takes me a long time to respond."

"Well learn, take the effort to fucking learn dad, I ask your advice, I want your guidance and you have not got a clue, you do not know how to parent, your meant to be my dad, you are meant to protect, love and support me. You are meant to give me advice dad, why can you not do that!" at this point I was slamming my hand into the wall and yelling down the phone at him, if he had of been in front of me I would have beat him to a pulp.

"Son I can't hear you, the line is breaking up son"

"Don't you dare put the fucking phone down on me!" I shouted just before the line went dead.

My hand shaking with anger I frantically pressed the call back button.

As my phone buzzed in my hand I pressed the green button and put it to my ear.

"Sorry about that son, the line went dead, it was breaking up"

"Son, son! Don't call me fucking son! You put the phone down on purpose, you can-not even have a phone call, you can't tell me the truth, all I wanted was the truth and I would have given you another chance"

"I am sorry that you feel that way, I am sorry I was not what you wanted nor expected." Dad responded, keeping his voice as calm as he could, however I could hear him forcing anger down, so he did not explode and start shouting back.

I however was not forcing any anger down, I let it go, and continued to completely let it out.

"Feel that way! Feel! You are meant to be my dad. Do not ever contact me again, and if I see you near me or my family I will fucking kill you myself. I will rip you from limb to limb."

"I would not do any of that anyway son, I am sorry that you feel this way" my dad responded, almost in a patronising tone.

"You have been warned" I shouted, before putting down the phone.

Chapter 21.

<u>Nearly dead.</u>

I can safely say that that was the last time I saw the therapist, and the last time and only time I spoke to my dad. Being honest that experience scared the shit out of me. But even though my treatment was not finished, and I should have continued with it, the flashbacks were gone, and have not returned since.

It was 8 months into living in the terrace house in the town of Macclesfield. Things had gone downhill fast with the landlady, we paid our rent every month and we kept the house clean and tidy, we had moved in to her house and completed for free £2500 pounds worth of work to get it to a habitable standard, one that it was not in when we moved in.

Using my skills and the staff that I had at the time I had gutted the building, kitchen and bathroom I had ripped out, for free. Skip after skip, full of stuff I had loaded and paid for, me and my staff, for free. We had bought the cooker, the cooker hood, the beam above the fireplace I had personally bought and spent 2 days sanding and turning it into a beam suitable to be above a fireplace. 2 heavy large pine type doors I had removed from the pantry area and spent a further 2 days sanding old paint off them and replacing the doors.

Linda the lady I had trusted and the lady that had had me call her Mum for the last 8 months had turned on me and my family. She had suddenly decided, completely out of the blue, that she did not want us in the property anymore, she had decided after everything that we had done for her to believe the lying, twisted and manipulative psychotic neighbour over us.

The neighbour that told her that I had smashed the windows in his greenhouse, yet he had not contacted the police to report this?

 The one that stood at the end of the garden watching my wife through the window as she washed the pots. The one that sat in his car directly outside our house to perv on my wife and kids in the front garden. The one that told my father in law that he was going to smash my face in for breaking his greenhouse windows and for making noises when doing work to the house.

 I remember that day clearly, the father in law was working for myself at the time. We were working in a 1-million-pound house that had featured on a channel four documentary, my customers phoning me a week before filming was due, telling me that they wanted myself over the channel four producer's cleaners to do the cleaning work in their house as they trusted our company more. Regarding the father in law, it had taken him all day to pluck the courage up to tell myself that he had been speaking to him and had threatened to do harm to myself.

 "Thank you for telling me, I will be having words" I had replied that day.

I was simmering as I drove home that day, my nose began to itch as I dropped Sophie s dad off at his house, I breathed in deeply to try and calm myself down as I pulled up outside my house. Pissed that I was. However, I was sensible, the guy was an old man, yet a lot bigger than myself and looked like he could handle himself, I had to be smart, professional about the situation.

As I walked down the drive way I counted down from ten in my head, if I lost it I would start swinging and I would not stop, I knew that from all the pent-up anger that was locked away from my past. I envisioned myself being took away in handcuffs, my wife and children crying at the front door, leaving them living next door to the monster I had just beaten to a pulp. The front page of the Macc express would read. 'Young business man beats up defenceless old man' it would not be true; the paper never gets the story right. But still, I would be known as a thug and a bully, that I would not have.

As he answered the door I took a step back and smiled.

"Hi how we doing, look just a quick one, have me and you got a fucking problem? Apparently, you said you were going to punch me in the face to a family member, if you have a

problem you need to at least have the balls to knock on my fucking door."

I stood strong, yet at the same time shocked at what had come out of my mouth, that was not what I had intended to say at all, but I guess the pent-up anger was showing itself.

He twisted his thick dog lead between his hands as he looked down at myself from the step, he seemed angry yet at the same time anxious.

"No, I didn't say that to anyone, but me and you have got a problem" he retorted gripping the blue and black dog lead even tighter between his hands.

"Right, So, what's the problem that we have so we can resolve it, and why have you not had the balls to knock on my front door and fucking talk to me about it instead of threatening me behind my back?"

I asked, annoyed at his arrogance.

"You have rubbish in your garden and you have rats, you need to get rid of it, I have reported you to environmental health, also if you want a fucking problem I will give you a fucking problem." He said angrily as he stepped forward.

I took a step back, annoyed at his advance, but at the same time trying to stay professional.

"Firstly, the rubbish in my garden has number one, got fuck all to do with you, number two, does not have rats in it, and number 3 is being removed weekly. Now if you do not mind, I would prefer it if you did not threaten myself behind my back, and if you have something that you want to say then knock on my door." I replied as I turned to walk away, at this point I was angry and had to remove myself from the situation before I did something that I could regret in the near future.

"I watch you" the old man's voice sent a chill up my spine as I got to the black metal gate at the top of his front garden.

"Excuse me" I said as I turned back to look at him.

"I see you when you leave the house at 3 am in the morning, I watch you out of my window. I also watch your wife from my garden, your children, and you. You will never get away, I am always watching you."

I closed my eyes as my brain absorbed what it was that he had just said, I felt sickened to the stomach, as my stomach knotted in anger, I did the wises thing that I could think of, I walked away and back into my house. As I closed my front door I could feel the anger bubbling from my stomach and up into my chest. I could envision myself smashing his face into the brick wall of his house as the skin removed itself from his cheek bones.

After that, it was not long before we left, we had to, we had no choice. My mum, that she had titled herself, bombarded us with different letting agents, txt messages, solicitor's

letters and phone calls, she wanted to change tenancy contracts which we refused to do. She accused us of burning plastic in the fire place and she accused us of not keeping the house clean and tidy. The house was always clean and tidy.

When we finally moved it was with excitement and we were determined to make a fresh start. She was a bully and we no longer wanted to live in that house, the house that I had spent hours and hours cleaning, painting, everything. She had ripped us off, I was pissed, pissed that I had let it happen and pissed that she had abused our trust in her. Pissed that I had let another "Mother" into my life. A mother figure in which I so needed, wanted, another mother figure in which ripped my heart in two and threw it on the floor in front of me. A mother figure in which I would have done anything for. I was again a broken man.

After that we moved into a house that we have turned into a home. I have a job that I love, and I live with people and work with people that I love.

However, it was August 2014 when I nearly lost it all, the date that Robin Williams hung himself.

On that morning, (very close to that date) I went to work at 7am and came home from work at about 7pm. I had had a busy day working on a customer's garden preparing it for flagging. I had then gone to a friend's house and bought a washing machine down a flight of stairs for him. I was back to smoking cigars as my stress levels had risen over the last few weeks and I needed a release. Alcohol was not an option, I knew if I became hooked on that stuff I could kiss goodbye to anything that was good in my life.

That night I got home and did not feel very well, my chest felt tight and I felt somewhat faint. So, I took myself to bed, as soon as my head hit the pillow I was asleep, an exhaustion like no other, one in which engulfed myself, body and soul, one in which I could not fight, one in which I had never experienced before.

The following morning, I awoke, my chest still felt tight, but I forced myself to sit up in bed and told the wife that I would be ok after a few minutes. Running through what it was that I had to do that day in my head I decided that it was time for me to get up. As I swung my legs over the side of the bed and stood up my knees collapsed from under me and I fell face first onto the wooden floor. I pulled myself to my hands and knees and tried to take a breath in, but it was hard to do, there was a crushing sensation in my chest and it felt as though someone was squeezing my lungs and throat from inside preventing me from breathing. Sophie helped me stand up and one step at a time we walked down the stairs and into the living room, by now I was trying not to panic but I could not breath.

Lying on the sofa I tried to slow my breathing, but my chest seemed to tighten every-time I took a breath in making it nearly impossible for me not to panic. In addition to this the room had begun to spin, and I had become very sweaty and clammy on my hands and chest area especially.

In the car on the way to A and E I clutched at my chest as if trying to pull my lungs apart to enable air to get in, curled in a ball one hand on the dash and the other pulling at my chest I took a shallow breath in, my vision now blurry, as if I had been drinking heavily.

The passenger door opened, and I felt small but strong arms grab my hand, my wife helped me step out of the car as we arrived at the hospital. As I looked up towards the entry of A and E I suddenly felt a sharp stabbing pain in the left side of my chest and back, my knees buckled, my vision now blurrier then before I felt myself hit the concrete pathway with force, now lying on my side I realised that my chest had closed completely, and I could not breath at all.

I felt a foamy substance leave my mouth and my body started to violently shake, I had lost control of my body. Upon hearing feet rushing towards me I managed to force my head to look up, I saw 2 ambulance crew running, I followed my wife with my eyes as she appeared at the side of my children, a look of horror on their face, a look I will never forget.

I closed my eyes as I felt a sudden surge of euphoria close around me and flow through my body.

Opening them slightly I took one last glance at my children and the wife. I felt myself separate from my body that was still behaving in an uncontrollable and erratic manner, there was no audio and there was no feeling in body anymore, no pain, no nothing, just an incredible feeling of euphoria and acceptance, acceptance of death. This was the end, this is how I was going to die, outside on the concrete, outside the A and E department of a hospital.

Suddenly I felt strong arms lift me from the floor and a female voice tell me to try and lift my head that was rolling about on its own as if it was not attached to my neck. The pain was back and my breathing none existent still.

"Name, age, any recreational drugs taken? The paramedic asked my wife in rapid fire, her replies I struggled to hear as I was still trying to breath.

On the A and E bed in the rhesus department of the hospital I was swarmed with doctors and nurses whom pinned me to the bed and stuck a needle in me with a drip feed attached to it.

After a few minutes, my breathing returned to normal and the pains in my chest stopped. The doctor stood at the foot of my bed and looked at me disapprovingly, as if I should not have been there.

"What is happening to me?" I asked him panicked as I gripped at my chest, it, becoming tight again.

"you have had a panic attack, it's all in your head, you are fine" the doctor replied sternly.

I feel like it is something worse than a panic attack, my gut tells me otherwise, so why do the doctors words hurt so much? Why do they make me feel so worthless and not good enough?

A nurse comes over and takes my heart beat with a machine, she also takes my blood pressure.

I hear her tell the doctor that my heart beat is irregular and that she is concerned, it breaks out into an argument with the doctor and the nurse. The doctor being adamant that I have just had a panic attack and the nurse determined that there is something worse. About an hour passes and I am let out from hospital with instructions to make an appointment at the GP. Instructions from the nurse as the doctor just wanted me out of his rhesus room.

I go to the doctors a few days later. I feel determined to make sure that they double check everything, but, there is still a niggling in the back of my head, the doctors words not wanting to leave me so easily.

"It's all in your head!" Words I had heard so many times as a child, now I was hearing them again, but as an adult. I was angry, embarrassed and hurt as I walked into the doctor's room.

A few weeks after visiting the doctor I was sat waiting in the waiting room, waiting for a treadmill test.

As I walked into the room I took a glance at the treadmill and then at the female nurse and the male cardiologist. They gestured for me to sit on a seat whilst they put sticky tabs on my chest to get a heart reading before I got onto the treadmill.

After a few seconds, the nurse and the cardiologist exchanged nervous glances.

"I will be back in a minute, you are not getting on the treadmill your heart reading is abnormal."

He explained, clearly trying to remain calm and professional, but failing. I felt a sense of relief as I watched the man exit the room, a relief that I was not being dramatic, and it was not all in my head, but then I also felt a sense of dread, there was something wrong with my heart, and if there was something that wrong was it going to kill me?

As I walked through the waiting room I glanced at my wife sat there waiting for me, the women that had stood with me through thick and thin, and now I was here, potentially going to give her some of the worse news she was going to get. Smiling at her weakly I followed the nurse into the scan room, as instructed I lay on my side as the women put jelly on the scan machine before rubbing it on my chest area and looking at a monitor, the screen she turned away from me and instructed me to face the opposite way.

"Have you got children?" she asked as I felt her stop with the machine, and study the screen whilst applying pressure to the same spot on my chest.

I grunted in pain as she pushed the scanning machine into my chest bone.

"Oh sorry" she said releasing pressure.

I told her about my children as she had asked, but I could not help but feel she was asking me because she had found something.

I was right, it was about a week later when I was told that my left ventricle in my heart had weakened and had swollen, opening and causing the heart to pool blood and not pump it around the body properly. Medication is the temporary fix that I am on now, it's there to help the heart and slow the failing process down, it is there to make the heart beat as normally as possible.

I was relieved to find out that my gut instinct was correct, yet I was annoyed that the A and E doctor had not listened to me and had dismissed that it could have been anything other than a panic attack because of my age at the time. The doctor had a very closed mind. In this case it could have been the difference between life and death.

This now brings me to the end of my life story, for now.

The reason I have written my autobiography first is to give you an idea of where I have come from and the kind of life that I have lived, when I show you methods of coping and succeeding in this world I am doing it from a place of complete genuine intent, and I am guiding you as someone whom has been there, someone who has done that and someone whom at one point seriously thought that he was useless and pathetic. So much so that I was willing to inflict severe harm to myself.

I have come a long way in a short space of time, so can you.

It is time to access the power of you.

<u>Accessing the power of you.</u>

<u>Chapter 1.</u>

<u>Being honest with yourself.</u>

Now I have read a few self-help books, I have also read blogs, listened to audio files and invested time into changing my life for the better. I am also part of a mind mastery group that I pay for every month so that I can better my own life to help support others.

So far however (even though the groups and other material has been amazing in my growth as a person) I have not heard anyone of these people advice what I am advising here.

That advice is this.

To start your journey of self-discovery, to harness your inner potential and to change your life for the better, you need to do this one thing.

Be honest with yourself, be completely 100 percent without doubt honest with yourself.

You see we tell ourselves lies continuously to feed our ego and our self-elusions.

For example, we may say internally

"That it is ok, I only drank one bottle of wine last night, it's not that much."

This as we know is a lie, not only because we also know that for the last 5 nights we have been downing a bottle a night to try and cope with a bad breakup. "But its ok, "its only temporary" we tell ourselves. This makes us feel better about ourselves, our excuses, (a bad breakup) and our self-destructive behaviours, (excessive drinking) in which we try and reason with the excuse.

However, If, you are here, you have already made the decision to change and improve your life for the better, apply these strategies and follow this book step by step and you are guaranteed to get results, but only if you apply the strategies offered.

So, let's get started, by being honest with yourself and taking responsibility for your life, meaning let's take control and act!

Being completely honest with ourselves does not mean blowing smoke up our arses and telling ourselves lies to make ourselves feel better, it is about being real and even if it hurts still being honest with ourselves.

So, without hesitation let's do this!

Grab yourself a pen and some paper, and draw a chart like the one on the following page. The examples given in the chart are real life things that have happened to myself and real-life behaviours and thought processes that I used to display, I just wish back then I had someone to show myself what I am showing you now!

What behaviour/thought process do you do/have that do not serve you. Being 100% raw and honest with yourself no matter how painful.	What are the consequences in the negative to this behaviour/thought pattern.	What is the positive intention of the behaviour or thought pattern? What is it trying to do for you?
That I am not good enough.	I do not try to do anything, I become depressed.	To stop me from trying which in turn protects me from the potential of failure and rejection.
That no one will ever love me.	I do not try and make new friends or spend time with family.	This protects me from rejection.
Burning myself.	I have sore and damaged skin that could become infected.	This makes me feel alive and brings me to the present moment taking my thoughts away from

		how much of a failure I believe I am.
How can we teach our mind to serve us better? How can we change our behaviour patterns?	What are the gains to changing my behaviour patterns? How does this impact my life and my future?	5 things I can do right now in this moment, that I can do consistently daily, to start my transformation for a better life.
Look for examples in the past when we did feel good enough, worthy and loved.	I will be able to achieve my goals and dreams, I will be able to become emotionally and financially abundant.	1/ Realise and tell myself that I am awesome, and I am good enough. 2/ Tell myself that I am loved.
Decide today to stop the unwanted behaviour as it does not serve us, go and get help and advice from as many places as I can.	I will no longer have sore or damaged skin which I must hide, and which has the potential of becoming infected. I realise that I am loved and	3/ Spend time with people, get a hobby and invest time and energy in that. 4/ Decide today to stop unwanted

		behaviour.
See a therapist if needed.	Wanted in this world.	5/Write down negative feelings and rip up the paper and throw it away.

By making a chart like the one above and writing these things down It will start to become clear where you are in the now and were you need to be going in the future. I know that it is painful being so honest with yourself and stripping away your ego but once you do this then this opens opportunity to change.

It came to a point in my life where I walked into my living room one morning, and in there was empty beer bottles, a 1 litre empty bottle of gin and the place stunk of alcohol, in addition to this my computer was infected with viruses due to the amount of porn that I was watching, and my leg was burning from the self-harm that I had inflicted upon myself 2 days previous.

That was my wake-up call, it was what made me decide to change my ways. That chart above is like what happened in my mind that day, I hated were I was going and what I was doing, I had to decide to change and I did. That day, in that moment I thought to myself I must change. And I did, and that is all it takes, it takes one moment to decide that you no longer want to live that way, you no longer want to be in your issue and live with your problems.

The first step is being honest with yourself with a no bullshit approach, the second step is to decide to change.

Chapter 2,

Teaching the subconscious mind.

So, you have made the decision to change, you have decided that you no longer want your issue, whether that be anxiety, depression, anger, alcoholism or self-harm. You have decided to change.

Well done!

Life can be hard, and our brain can make life harder, even though its intention is to try and protect us, what it does is in many cases end up self-sabotaging us.

We have the conscious, the part of the brain that we are aware off, then we have the subconscious. This is the part of the brain that is always listening and learning, it is also always receiving information passed down from the conscious part of the brain. The subconscious is also the part of the brain in which controls us and our behaviour in most circumstances putting us on automatic pilot without sometimes realising what we are doing, for example driving somewhere then getting there and not remembering how we got there. This is the part of the brain in which we must teach.

You see the subconscious brains job is to protect us. It does this by learning from its surroundings, our conscious thoughts and the way in which the biological body responds to situations, which in turn creates belief systems based upon how we felt in that situation.

So, for example,

When I was working for my adoptive
father, he used to shout at me in front of people and
down-talk me in front of people.

There was one time in which I have never forgotten. We
were outside his garage and he asked me to hook a
trailer up to a car, the trailer and the car where near each
other I just had to hook the trailer onto the towing ball. I
could not do it and I did not understand how it fitted
together. Instead of helping me and showing me how to
do it he stood and watched me, he then started shouting
at me in front of the customer and saying that I needed
to open my eyes and that I was stupid. This made me go
red in the face with embarrassment and shame and I felt
somewhat trapped in the situation. I could not see what
it was that he wanted me to do and every time I moved
to try and solve the problem he would shout "No"
making me freeze in position daring not to move.

It was in that moment that my subconscious mind
decided for me, and that decision was this. It decided
that I would have the belief system that I was not good
enough, and it also made the decision that it did not like
me being in situations where I was around customers
when Mark was around.

So, what did it do? Well to protect me it made me
believe I was not good enough, to protect me it made me
feel anxious whenever I saw a customer, it made me feel

sweaty and sick and light headed around customers when mark was around.

This was my subconscious way of keeping me away from a situation that it believed was a dangerous situation as I had not felt good when Mark had treated me like that in front of people.

So how do we retrain the brain to realise and disprove the belief system that we are not good enough?

There are 4 ways in which we can do this, and I suggest doing all 4 to get plenty of clarification and plenty of evidence to disprove the theory or the belief system that you are not good enough. The first way is to look in our past and think back to a time when we were good enough. This would normally be a time in which we did not have the issue, whatever that issue may be, for me personally it was anxiety around a certain situation. For you it could be anything, from depression, the feeling of not being good enough or feeling unworthy.

So, let's start to disprove that belief system in which you hold about yourself together. My belief system was that I was not good enough which then created anxiety. By asking questions we can start to look in our past and unpick the belief system which in turn creates a new way for us to be in this world.

Follow these 3 step by step guides below which in turn will change;

1/ Looking back into your past and changing the belief system that you are not good enough. (Or whatever belief system it is in which you hold these processes will work for all)

2/ You can also future pace the situation and the way in which we want to act and react in the situation.

3/ The relationship with the individual, whoever that may be in your life.

a/ either getting rid of the person out of your life.

b/ changing the way you think about the individual and act and react around them.

<u>1/ Looking back into your past and changing the belief system that you are not good enough. (Or whatever belief system it is in which you hold these processes will work for all)</u>

Now before Mark shouted at me in front of the customer did I feel good enough to be around customers?

Well, yes, I did feel good enough to be around customers.

Why in the positive did I feel good enough?

Well I used to be able to talk to customers without getting anxious feelings, I used to be able to answer their questions with ease and confidence and I used to be able to assist the customer in whatever it was that they needed.

Ok so straight away by asking a question we have come up with a time in the past when we felt good enough.

Now what I want you to do is sit down and close your eyes, when your eyes are closed what I want you to do is think about that time in which you were good enough, or in my case when I was good with customers. I want you to go deep in that thought, think about what you saw, what you heard and what you felt in that situation, go deep in your mind and in that memory and really feel what it was that you felt. Remember how confident you were, how you acted and reacted to that situation with such strength and confidence.

When you are really deep in that thought and you have the intense feeling of total confidence and strength I want you to open your eyes and as soon as your eyes are open I want you to write down how you are feeling, what you saw and heard, what you felt in your body and were in your body it was that you felt it, repeat this process daily for 6 weeks to really strengthen that belief system and create the connection between your conscious and subconscious thus teaching the subconscious a new way of being.

It is important that you follow the process and that you write down your feelings and the memory in detail as it will give you clarification and will start to disprove the belief system in which you currently hold about yourself.

Future pacing.

Future pacing your life to change a belief system.

What is future pacing?

Future pacing to me is something that we already do as humans, but many of us future pace in the negative.

Have you ever been going somewhere, or an event has been coming up and instead of looking forward to the event/place you are visiting you have instead played out scenarios in your head of all the things that could possibly go wrong?

Such as, "What if the car breaks down?" whilst imagining you having to pull over whilst the car pummels smoke from under the bonnet?

"What if we run out of money?" whilst you picture yourself scavenging for change in the bottom of your purse or wallet whilst a long que of people behind you in the supermarket wait impatiently?

"What if he/she does not like me?" whilst imagining being ignored from the man/women of your dreams as they stare at their phone whilst you awkwardly sit there in the busy pub with your hands clasped nervously around your drink.

Although these in a way can be useful thoughts if you act upon them, for example getting breakdown cover just in case the car should break down. They other than that are not very useful to ourselves, the future pacing in the negative can be a nerve wrecking experience and can lead to us creating self-sabotaging behaviours.

However, if we teach our brain to future pace in the positive and we create a habit by doing this every night then we can direct our brains to create a positive emotional response when you think of the following day, or a situation that in the past may have filled you with dread and fear, you will be filling the body and mind instead with positive emotions which will help drive you forward and feel and experience positive vibes which you will in turn give out to the world around you.

So how do we do this?

Every night before you go to bed I want you to either sit somewhere comfy or just lie down in your bed whatever suits you. And whilst you are there I want you to close your eyes and I want you to watch from a third person perspective yourself, so in other words I want you to imagine yourself getting up in the morning, making your food, getting ready for work, whatever it is that you do during the day step by step. So, from first thing in the morning until you go to bed at night, I want you to go through your day in your head, but thinking about the following day, So, if its Tuesday night then go through Wednesday in your mind.

There is a twist however, when you are going through your day in your mind I want you to imagine yourself acting and reacting to situations in a way that makes you feel empowered, so for example if you feel nervous around your boss at work, I want you to see yourself reacting to her/him in the most confident way ever! Watch yourself as you speak to her/him with purpose, confidence and watch yourself as you stand tall and look the person directly in the eyes as you are speaking in a clear and directional tone driven by purpose and strength.

As you finish your working day watch yourself as you leave the place of work knowing you have had a positive day and have been constructive, watch as the person whom is you strives and achieves excellence in every part of their life.

Watch as that person climbs into bed at night time, tired from a successful day but happy in their successes. Then open your eyes as you realise you are that person.

This is a must on positive transformation, it takes time to create a habit but be sure to hold yourself accountable, this book is here to help you transform your life and this can be done but it is going to take commitment from yourself. You can do this!

<u>Changing your relationship with an individual, or cutting them off?</u>

   Now this one is massive, you can either change the relationship you have with someone, or you can choose to cut them off.

   There's 3 ways to deal with toxic people, and I say toxic because the kind of person which I am thinking about is the kind of person whom is unpredictable in their behaviour, or the kind of person that brings you down by just being in the same room as you, there energy being that negative that you feel drained after spending any amount of time around them.

<u>Number 1.</u>

 Show them how to be in this world.

   This can be hard to do but with practice it can be done, I know that it is not something that I could achieve around Mark even though it is a powerful process, I am just being honest, it works around some people and not around others.

   That is why I cut Mark out of my life.

   This is how we do this process, before you go and see this negative person I suggest that you put yourself in a peak state of emotion. We can do this through meditation, either sitting in a room in silence or with relaxing music on for 10 minutes right before you leave to go and see this individual.

Whilst you are sitting there just clear your mind of any negative thoughts, imagine yourself being flooded with happiness and strength on an emotional and bodily level. Imagine yourself as you, breath, breathing in strength, courage and love and when you breathe out breathing out negative thoughts and emotions. Clearing your mind from worries and concerns from the future and clearing the ghosts of the past. Be in the moment, there breathing and hearing what you can hear and feeling what you can feel.

You can either do this exercise by listening to meditative music, sitting in silence, or following this link and listening to the create your day track and or my feel-good podcast.

https://www.patreon.com/mentalhealthsupport

These links are completely free to use and there is also other links there in which are accessible and free to yourselves.

When you see the individual drown out their negativity with love and support, combat their rudeness and negative outlook on life with positivity, in some cases change the subject if the individual is intent on being negative.

Number 2 distance yourself.

Sometimes, just sometimes, it does not matter how many self-help books we read, (including myself) how many times we try with somebody or how much positivity you flood yourself and them with, including changing your energy (emotional state) so it is in a peak state to override their negative energy.

Just sometimes no matter what you do the other person does not want or is unwilling to change their behaviour, and that is the time when we must realise that we must take responsibility for our own happiness and if that means distancing ourselves from an individual whether that be a family member, friend or even work colleague, then it must be done.

I am not saying here that you must completely cut them out of your life, there are situations that make this hard to do, for example an ex-girlfriend/boyfriend whom you have a child with would be practically impossible to cut them off completely if you are picking up your son or daughter of a weekend and must communicate with each other regularly.

You can however distance yourself, reducing the communication to texting instead of talking on the phone, making sure all communication is just about the child and not getting into any long-winded discussions about anything irrelevant.

Then you have situations such as your parents. Even though I have cut mine off altogether I understand that some of you may not feel like you can do that even if they do drive you mad. Again, you can distance yourself by seeing them less often, instead of going once a week go once a month. In certain circumstances if they are always knocking on your door unwelcomed and you feel obliged to let them in, then move to a new house or pretend you are not in. This is something that myself and my wife had to do with certain members of our family and it has worked.

It has been like a weight has been lifted of our shoulders, distancing yourself certainly works.

Number 3 cut them off.

Finally, however, sometimes there are people in our life that make us so miserable that you must decide to either stay the way you are, whether that be being in a romantic relationship with that individual or whether that being in a working situation, you can either stay miserable, or make drastic changes to your life which in the long term will benefit you and possibly benefit them. Either way you are responsible for your happiness and no matter what anyone says you do not have to spend your life in a situation living with someone that makes you miserable. If it's in a working situation get a new job or set up your own business, if it's in a relationship then leave. Change is the key to happiness.

Sometimes you must just cut people out of your life.

You deserve to be happy.

Chapter3.

Taking on Anxiety.

Let's talk about anxiety,

Anxiety is the fear of the future, anxiety can be explained using the analogy of the snake, if you follow my face-book page you will have seen this before, but it is good to recap.

There is a picture of a rope in a book, the brain, your brain projects an image onto the rope, an image of a snake, the brain thinks that the rope is a snake, this then creates an emotional response, "fear" in many cases especially if you have a phobia snakes.

The fact is that there is nothing to be frightened of, the brain has created the image and project it onto the rope to protect you.

The brain has seen the worst-case scenario and frightened you to protect you.

Guess what? This is exactly what anxiety does.

To overcome anxiety or to at least relieve its symptoms, we need to follow some simple steps to help rewire our minds.

There are 3 steps to take to help relieve anxiety.

Step 1. creating a gratitude journal.

This may sound as Joseph Clough would say a bit "woo la la" but it is essential in the path of emotional freedom and transformation.

Either get yourself a piece of paper, I suggest a note pad though so that you can look back on other gratitude notes that you have made. But a pen and piece of paper will do.

Then every night before you go to bed write down, (it's very important that you write this down as the process of writing it down will help your conscious pass this information down to your subconscious which will then create a new way of being and a new behaviour.) 5 things in which you are grateful for. These can be anything, from being grateful that you are alive, that you can walk if you can walk, that you can and have food and water. Maybe you are grateful that you have got a house or a flat if you have somewhere to live. Maybe you are grateful that you have a job if you have a job?

Maybe you are grateful that you are reading this book?

These are the types of things that you could write down in your daily gratitude journey.

This will over time create a habit and your mind will start to look for things in your daily life in which you can be grateful for, which will start to shift your emotional, mental and biological approach to life. Changing the way in which you feel and think about yourself and the world around you.

I also suggest writing at the end of the list writing or saying to yourself "I love you" even if you do not believe it at first your subconscious mind will be listening, and this will also create a new way of behaving and thinking about yourself.

Step 2. Future pacing your day.

Refer to page 169 were I have described how to future pace your life, this should then in addition to doing the gratitude exercise start to help you and your subconscious to work together to create a life with less anxiety and more emotional freedom.

It is all about changing perspective and if you and your subconscious work together then you can change the way in which your body and mind act and react to life challenges.

You can change the way in which you perceive the world and by following these processes the challenges or situations in the past, in which you maybe once feared or became anxious around, you will be able to approach in a more confident manner coming from a place of contentment and happiness.

Step 3. Changing your state instantly.

This is one of my favourite techniques in the self-help world and one in which I have used many times myself. One that 100 percent works!

We are human, and there are times in our life in which we enter a state of emotion in which does not help us, whether that emotion be anxiety, anger, frustration, any negative emotion in which we can think of.

Now don't get me wrong, there are times when these emotions are good, and we should listen to them and look deep within ourselves and ask what it is that they are trying to tell us?

For example, are we angry because of our own behaviour and actions? Or are we angry because of a situation in which we have been stuck in for a long time and one in which we need to get out of, is the emotion telling us that it is time to change?

These are questions in which we need to ask ourselves, especially if we are facing regular negative emotions. They are normally telling us that something needs to change.

But there are times in which we need to change our emotional state instantly, such as if we are in a situation where there is a possibility that we could lose our Job if we become angry and let the emotion take over the moment and we verbally or physically lash out in anger.

So how do we change our emotional state instantly?

The way we do this is to create a neuro connection in our body and mind. We can do these 2 ways and I suggest getting into the habit of doing both.

The first way is to close your eyes and think back to a moment in the past in which you felt happy or excited. Think back to a moment in your life in which you experienced a positive emotion, one that really sticks with you.

In your mind I want you to see what you saw and feel what you felt, once you are in that positive mental state and you have them feelings in your body and mind I want you to gently, yet firmly enough to feel it. Press your thumb and your middle finger (index finger together). Hold them together when you are in the peak state of that emotion, when the emotion starts to subside release the finger and the thumb.

The other way in which you can do this which will strengthen the neuro connections within your body and mind is to press your finger and thumb together when you are in the present moment and are experiencing a peak state of emotion. So, for example if you are doing something in which you enjoy and are experiencing a positive emotion just press your finger and thumb together and hold it there for a few seconds before releasing it. This will tell your mind and body that when you press your finger and thumb together you want to experience an emotion in which is positive.

So, if you are in a situation in which your boss at work is really pissing you off, instead of telling him or her to go and F### off, (we have all been close to it, iv even done it) and potentially losing your job.

You can instead press your finger and thumb together in which will create a connection to your brain, your brain will go, "Oh, last time we did this, we felt like this" and your mind will then release the endorphins and create the biological response which will in turn change your emotional state instantly.

Step 4. Writing this piece of literature down, putting it somewhere in which you can see it and reading it every day to remind you what anxiety is and that you are in control!

About anxiety,

Being in a body, one that responds to situations with fear, the mind creating horrific images of what things could/might happen, when you have anxiety you live in the future, fearing the future yet living in the future, living in fear. Always worrying what if? not giving the mind body and soul time to rest, continuedly alert, fearful and nervy.

The mind racing images flashing, and heart pumping heard, you feel faint and breathing shallow, even thinking about a situation can create an anxious reaction.

But wait, stop, it does not have to be this way, anxiety is your friend. "what?" I hear you say.

It's time to change, let's ask anxiety what it is that it is trying to tell us? What it wants?

Ultimately it wants to keep us safe but does not know how so we need to teach it.

To do this, we need to change perception.

Have you heard about the snake and the rope?

It's a picture of a rope yet the first impression we get of it when we see it is that it is a snake, the mind creates a snake from the shape of the rope, the mind sees the bad in the world before it sees the good, it sees the potential danger. It does this to protect us, just like what anxiety does.

It superimposes a negative and dangerous tint onto a none dangerous situation to keep us safe when there is no danger.

Write down a situation in detail, a situation where you feel anxious, think about it in detail and think about how you feel, think, and act and react to the situation. Every little detail, write everything.

Then write down on a separate piece of paper the way you want to be in this world, the way you want to act and react and how you want to feel. Imagine having emotional freedom. Imagine yourself confident, seeing and doing it!

Then the following day repeat the process but just writing down how you want to be in the world, how you

want to act and react and feel, how amazing you are
going to be.

Do this every day, create a habit.

Chapter 4.

Tackling depression.

Depression, the word depression itself is a heavy word. I am depressed, I have depression, I suffer from depression.

These are all words that are used by people whom experience this awful disease which is not a visible illness, just like any mental health issue. It's not visible so the general conception is that it is not real, even when this could not be further from the truth.

In my opinion being immobilised by depression is one of the most real and one of the hardest things to overcome. But it can be overcome, and this is the main thing to realise, depression can be overcome.

I remember lying in my bed when I lived alone in the flat, the covers feeling like a lead weight and my body near enough impossible to move due to feeling that low. Like a lead weight was in my chest I just lay there, looking up at the ceiling, sometimes getting the strength to look up at the window in the corner of the room. The wooden slated blinds the only thing stopping myself from being over looked by the shop across the road. I could hear the scum of the town shouting outside as I lay there, to exhausted and to depressed to move. Believing that I was not good enough, not worth anything and believing that I was never going to be loved or wanted. I was skint, almost homeless and I could see no way out. I hated my job, I hated myself and I hated my life. I looked down at the red marks on my wrist from the elastic band, then closed my eyes and fell asleep. Along with this depression came an addiction to alcohol, self-harm, horrific nightmares and an aggressive attitude towards not only myself but others.

That was my experience of depression, and that is where we should start.

The linguistics in which we use when we describe our situations have a massive effect on our progress and recovery.

You see I experienced depression, I did not suffer depression, or if you currently are experiencing depression, then that Is exactly what you are doing, experiencing it. You see if we experience something then we can move on and progress, but if you are in the mind frame that you are suffering from depression then you are putting your brain into a victim mentality.

A victim mentality makes us become stuck in the situation, in which we are in as someone whom suffers something cannot move forward, were as if we experience something then we can move forward.

You also must realise that even if you feel like you do you are not depression; a lot of people say that they are depression, (and many other mental illnesses) they identify themselves as that depressed person, that anxious person or that angry person.

But depression is not your identity, you are not depression. "How am I not depression?" I hear you ask.

Well, when you last watched that movie that made you laugh and smile where you depressed then? Well no because you were experiencing happiness. So how can you always be depressed? How can you identify as depressed when in that moment you were happy?

When you smelt that smell that took you back in time in your mind to a happier time in your life, when you were thinking about that time and you smiled with fond memories, were you depressed then?

Of course, you were not depressed, you were happy, possibly nostalgic also, but you were not depressed.

Do you see what we are doing here? We are breaking down the belief system that you are nothing but depressed, you are in fact a continues fluctuating energy of emotion.

Now I know how hard it is to reach out for help, I know how hard it is to admit to yourself that you have a problem, that you are depressed, it's even harder to reach out for help, but the moment you do will be the moment that your life starts to change for the better.

You can reach out for help by picking up the phone and calling the Samaritans just for someone to talk to. Depending on where you are in the world will depend on what their number is this can be found on the internet. In England, it is 116123.

You can also reach out for assistance from myself and my team on 07725794002, (this is a txt service only and will be responded to by myself as and when I can so do not rely on this if it is an emergency) and by joining my Facebook group accessing the power of you were you have myself and several other admins (and other members) on hand ready and waiting to assist you in changing your life for the better and getting yourself onto a happy pathway of success.

We can also start battling depression by deciding to change, deciding that we are no longer going to participate in depression, we are no longer going to let this invisible disease pin us down and stop us from living our life, why would we let this horrible illness stop us from enjoying this short time that we have on this planet.

It all starts off with that one decision, the decision that says no more, this is my life and I am going to start taking it back.

There are a couple of exercises that I suggest strongly in this book.

Firstly, I would choose a day to start, that day being today, not tomorrow or next week, now. I would then get a pen and some paper and write down these 3 things, ultimately creating yourself a very short job list.

1. To write down daily 5 things in which you are Great-full for, this can be anything from being great-full that you can walk and talk to being great-full that you have a bed to sleep in and family that love you.

2. GO FOR A WALK!

Even if it is a short stroll get out of the house, change your environment, and when you walk make sure you walk with your head up and shoulders back, the way you hold yourself when you walk will determine the way in which you feel. Your mind and body are connected, get your body moving and your mind will follow suit.

3. keep going, keep writing down the things in which you are great-full for, keep consistent, go for a walk every day, speak to people, invest in time for yourself, invest in you. Tell yourself that you love yourself, even if you do not believe it at first, keep telling yourself it. Dig deep and take control, this is your life and you can, and you will beat this experience, remember that is all that this is, it's just an experience and you can and will come out of the other side. Also make sure that your social circle is one that is positive, it has people in it whom see the good in life. Join accessing the power of you group!

Looking at life from different perspectives and taking a step back.

So, when life gets us down and we can see no way out of the situation in which we are in, this is when this little trick will come in handy. Sometimes we can look at a situation for weeks on end and see no solution to the problem, and there is one reason for that. The reason is that we are looking at the problem from our own world view, from our own point of view. We are looking at a problem from one angle.

So, let's say that you are in a situation where your car has broken down, (a real-life problem I have faced as I am sure many other people have!) and you have got no money to get it repaired. Pay day is not for another week, yet between now and pay day you still need to get to work. Work is about 4 miles away in distance, and Monday is here soon, it is Sunday afternoon and you are beginning to work up a sweat as you do not have a clue what you are going to do.

The first thing that you must do is take a step out of that situation and become the observer of yourself. It is so easy to let your mind and body consume you in stressful situations, by observing the self you are pulling your mind and body away from the unintentional victim mentality.

The mentality of "ahhh, what am I going to do!" and "Why is it always me?" we have all been there.

If when you are in a situation like this one you close your eyes and see yourself looking through your eyes, but at yourself, so watching as the observer. The observer of the self, not only will you disconnect from the stresses and strains of the emotions in which you are experiencing in that time, but you will allow yourself to see the issue from a different perspective.

So, whilst we are observing the self and looking at the way we are acting and reacting to the situation you will probably see that you are not responding to the stressful situation in the way in which you would like to. By observing the self, you can decide that you want to react in a calmer manner and as you watch yourself just imagine watching as the person in which you are watching calms down and takes a seat on the settee. Watch as the person, meaning you sits down on the seat and breathes in and out slowly throughout their nose calming themselves down to the point in which they are in a relaxed state of mind and body.

As this happens and the person in which you are watching is now calm I want you to realise that you feel calm within yourself. Your mind and body feel at piece as you now make the decision to tackle this problem from a completely different angle and outlook in life.

As you watch the person sitting on the settee I want you to have some fun as you come up with the solution to the problem.

So, we can start by asking questions such as. "What would person A do in this situation?"

For me personally person "A" could be a family member or friend in which I respect, or it could even be a famous actor or actress in which I respect, for example Jason Stathern. So, I could ask the question, "What would Jason Stathern do in this situation? Apart from shoot shit up and kick the shit-out of people what would he do?

This then changes your mind frame and ultimately you are asking your subconscious to come up with answers and you are asking your subconscious to look at the issue with a different worldview, so the world view of Jason Stathern.

Believe it or not your mind will then start to create a whole new set of answers and resolutions to the situation in which you are in, resolutions that you would have never have thought of without changing your world view.

In addition to this you can have some serious fun with it and ask things such as what would my pet dog think? What would my pet sheep or goat think? You see once we start to open the mind to a new way of being and seeing the world, your mind will start to open, and it will start to serve you in a more profound way.

This is the way in which we find solutions to problems in which we may have thought that we did not have access to the answers. By showing our brain and our mind a different way, it will then assist you in using that new-found way to find answers to an old or difficult problem.

Chapter 5.

Holding yourself accountable.

It does not matter how much content you read, or you listen to, if you want to change your life for the better then there is only one person in which can achieve that. That person is you, you and only you, and that person must act upon the content which they have read.

All the techniques which I have discussed in this book are techniques in which I have used myself, they are techniques in which I have followed through with on a continues bases, everything that is worth doing takes time and effort. When it comes down to your mental wellbeing and your life then you are the only person whom can make the changes that are necessary. You are also the only person whom can succeed in changing your life for the better.

So, my message to you is this, hold yourself accountable, if you want to change then you can do it, but you need to make sure that you do the techniques offered in this book.

Also join accessing the power of you if you so wish, which is a Facebook group in which is closely monitored by myself and in which we all rally round to support each other.

I also advise looking up other self-help gurus such as Joseph Clough whom has been someone whom has had a massive positive impact on my life. He made myself see the world in a completely different light, he saved my life, he was the one person whom had the right advice at the right time through his audio files and YouTube content.

Whatever situation you are facing at this present moment, it does not have to be the dictator of the direction of your life, there is always a way forward and there is always something in which you can do to change the course of your life.

Just be sure to hold yourself accountable by taking responsibility for your life.

Chapter 6.

On a philosophical level, realising that the self is separate from the biological body.

The philosophy in which I have adopted is that the self is separate from the human body.

Therefore, when we (I am purposely going to use the wrong linguistics here) suffer it is not actually the self that is suffering, it is the human body and mind.

Yes, the self is connected, and yes, the self may feel the pain in which the human body feels but on a deep level we can separate ourselves from this pain in which we feel.

The best way for me to explain this is when my heart used to cause myself great pain and when it used to make myself poorly before I was medicated for it which now controls it, I used to experience feeling poorly, light headed, being and feeling sick and shortness of breath to the extent in some cases that I stopped breathing. It was in one moment when I was lay on the pavement outside the accident and emergency department in which I realised that the self is separate from the body, the self, the core being that is creating this book, the being in which is me, my spirit, the sensation of my spirit beginning to leave my body and leaving behind the dying shell, the ultimate calmness in which engulfed myself in that moment, that is the self.

We can experience this when we realise that in the great scheme of life nothing matters, because in the end our human casing in which we are housed in is going to eventually stop working and we die on a human biological level, the self however, lives on, thus is not to say that we don't do stuff, and we don't still lead our life with passion, love, grit and determination.

It is however to say that we must carry the belief system (the human mind sometimes has a hard time comprehending what I am about to say so do not worry if your mind feels like it is about to explode!) which is we are nothing, yet we are everything.

Thus, meaning that we influence everything that in which we encounter, thus being on a biological level, a conscious and subconscious level and on a spiritual level.

We must ask ourselves when we come into contact with the things in which we influence then we must as much as we possibly can put into the world on a spiritual, biological and conscious level as much love as possible, in order to receive the love and positive vibes back.

On the flip side to this we also must remember that on a huge scale nothing really matters, when you experience this (which you can with practice) then you will understand to which why I am stressing the importance of the points in which I am making.

Live your life by giving out as much positive love and happiness into your internal and external world as possible.

But also realise that we are living in an infinite reality, meaning that even though the body may die, we all have what many refer to as a soul, an energy, and energy never dies, it cannot die, it may leave the human or animal body in which it inhabits but it moves onto a new and different level of consciousness, or maybe even a different spiritual plain, different world, or even a parallel universe. Possibly what we refer to as ghosts depending upon the situation in which the human body has passed.

We may in some circumstances come back as human beings, either way in the great scheme of things we are in an infinite reality, so always remember, nothing really matters in the long term as our body will eventually become old and die, leaving our souls, our energy, our basic form to pass onto the next chapter, giving us a chance to restart, giving us a chance to live our lives again whether that be in the spirit life or as an inhibiter of a body.

So to conclude this book, nothing matters in the long term, but it does not mean to say that we stop doing stuff, it does not mean to say that we stop trying, To succeed in this world we must live this life with passion, grit determination and love, creating and leaving behind memories of ourselves for our loved ones to look back fondly upon, for our legacy to be remembered by ones whom will remain on this conscious field in which we are all currently on, a legacy for us to be proud of, a legacy for us to possibly read about in years to come when we possibly return to the human world, yet at the same time realising that in the long term nothing really matters. Because our life is just a story book, a story book in which we create, make sure you make your story book a great read, one that which imprints itself upon others and one in which you have proven and shown to yourself that you have learned to love yourself which in turn has given you the confidence to love others.

Because that is what life is about, loving yourself, loving others and creating a profound and positive legacy, imprinting yourself on this world, before you move onto the reality in which follows this one, one in which we may never fully understand, yet one in which I know exists.

Joe.

If you enjoyed this book, then please look out for my work in the future as there are many more books that are due to be released from myself.

Also, please give myself a review.

Keep shining my friend.

Joseph Williamson.

Printed by Amazon Italia Logistica S.r.l.
Torrazza Piemonte (TO), Italy

10946165R00116